Microchild
Learning through LOGO

Macmillan Microcomputer Books

General Editor: Ian Birnbaum

Advanced Graphics with the BBC Model B Microcomputer
    Ian O. Angell and Brian J. Jones
Assembly Language Programming for the Acorn Electron
    Ian Birnbaum
Assembly Language Programming for the BBC Microcomputer
    Ian Birnbaum
Microchild—Learning through LOGO   Serafim Gascoigne
Using Your Home Computer
    Garth W.P. Davies

Also from Macmillan

Advanced Graphics with the Sinclair ZX Spectrum
    Ian O. Angell and Brian J. Jones
Advanced Programming for the 16 K ZX81   Mike Costello
Beginning BASIC   Peter Gosling
Continuing BASIC   Peter Gosling
Practical BASIC Programming   Peter Gosling
Program Your Microcomputer in BASIC   Peter Gosling
Codes for Computers and Microprocessors   P. Gosling and Q. Laarhoven
Microprocessors and Microcomputers — their use and programming
    Eric Huggins
The Sinclair ZX81 — Programming for Real Applications
    Randle Hurley
More Real Applications for the ZX81 and ZX Spectrum   Randle Hurley
Programming in Z80 Assembly Language   Roger Hutty
Digital Techniques   Noel Morris
Microprocessor and Microcomputer Technology   Noel Morris
The Alien, Numbereater, and Other Programs for Personal Computers — with
    notes on how they were written   John Race
Understanding Microprocessors   B.S. Walker
Assembly Language Assembled — for the Sinclair ZX81   Anthony Woods

Microchild
Learning through LOGO

Serafim Gascoigne

MACMILLAN

First published 1984 by
Higher and Further Education Division
MACMILLAN PUBLISHERS LTD
London and Basingstoke
Companies and representatives
throughout the world

Printed in Great Britain by
Camelot Press Ltd, Southampton

ISBN 0-333-37450-9

Contents

Preface

What is a micro? How does the micro affect your children's learning? At this very moment we are witnessing a technological revolution. By the year 2000 micros, like television, will be in nearly every home. Already the micro-computer and other electronic devices have entered the private lives of children. With the introduction of cable television, a vast quantity of computer software will be readily available. Such terms as pixel power, RAM and Artificial Intelligence will be familiar, everyday words.

Microcomputers are becoming smarter every year. Soon we will have intelligent machines that will be able to carry out routine jobs and give advice. Whether we look forward to these technological advances or not, the fact is that they are taking place, and at top speed!

How can we as parents, teachers, aunts and uncles — all of us who are involved with children — accommodate the demands of the new technology? What is the role of the school today? What sort of society are our children going to inherit by the time that they become parents? All these questions concern us both at home and in the classroom.

How can we prepare our children to face the challenge of the future? This book examines and attempts to provide practical answers to these questions through LOGO, a high-powered computer language written for children. Like King Canute, we cannot stop the sea, but we can harness this powerful technology and use it towards positive ends. LOGO enables children to come to terms with this technology. The microcomputer is seen not so much in terms of a sophisticated learning machine, but rather as a tool that can be used to aid and stimulate creative thinking.

Acknowledgements

I would like to thank John Lynch and David Perkin of the TANDY Corporation
for kindly providing equipment and technical assistance during the making of
this book and for the LOGO project in the classroom. Figure 9 is reproduced by
kind permission of Micropi and Tandy Corporation. My thanks also go to
Dr Gordon Mills of Bradford University for his support in this venture, and to
my friends in Class 6 at Moorfield First School in Bradford for their enthusiasm
and suggestions.

Last but not least, I wish to thank my family: Sarah-Frances for reading the
manuscript, exploring ideas in LOGO workshop, and for the drawings in this
book; Rachel, Gregory, Matthew and Xenia for trying out ideas at home.

PART 1: MICROCHILD

1 Microchild

Your child at school may be familiar with computers. He or she may talk about nothing else, driving you to distraction with micro-jargon. You may be confronted with such demands as 'Why can't I have one?' or 'Why did Tom's Dad buy him one for Christmas?' Perhaps you already have a micro at home, and are bombarded daily with the sound of space invaders and monster mazes. You might well say to yourself: 'I ought to be able to get much more out of this expensive piece of electronics? What kind of effect is it having on my child anyway?'

Your child may already be a microchild: one of those active youngsters who are in tune with the new micro-culture. If however your child or the children you teach are not yet familiar with computers, then they certainly will be in the near future. Already micros have entered the lives of many children and, as technology develops, the impact and the number of micros will increase.

The effect or impact that the micro is already having on my children at home and those that I teach may be illustrated by meeting three microchildren called Leon, Jasmin and Sharif.

Leon (nine years old) is intelligent. By 'intelligent' I do not mean academically successful. He is intelligent in that he is willing and able to tackle fresh problems. He displays an active and positive attitude towards learning. Leon questions everything and will spend hours or even days (if permitted) working on one task, be it a problem in Maths or an English project.

At the keyboard he works systematically, and at times doggedly, writing programs in Turtle Geometry. This entails driving an electronic animal, called a floor turtle, around the room, or moving a screen turtle on a TV screen. As the turtle* moves it can, if commanded, leave a pen trace, either on the screen or, in the case of the floor turtle, on a sheet of paper. Leon is always ready to have a go at the unknown. He does not rely on books for his answers. His understanding and interests are far more global than the school can provide.

---

*The original prototype was invented in the UK and was known as the 'tortoise'; it consisted of a domed box on wheels. Later, American 'turtles' were developed in conjunction with LOGO. The latest turtle produced in the UK operates by means of infra-red rays. This cordless animal also has 'eyes' which dim when the power supply is low. I personally would like to see the production of mini-turtles — brightly coloured animals about the size of a real tortoise; they could be called 'Lady Bugs'. Inventors please take note!

This has not always been the case. For nine years Leon has lived in the shadow of a bright, academically successful elder brother.

In an academic situation, Leon could be labelled 'bright but uncooperative'. From the very first day he set foot in the Nursery Class he became disruptive. He was a general nuisance to the teachers and the other children. This continued right through the classes of the first school until quite recently.

When I first met Leon, he stared at me for most of the day. Whenever I attempted to speak to him or other members of the class, he made 'funny' remarks. He also suffered from a nervous twitch. However after a term working with the computer, his twitch suddenly disappeared and at the same time he began to settle down to the normal routine of the school day.

Jasmin (eight years old) comes from Pakistan. She started learning English on arrival in this country, and continues to attend a special English-as-a-Second-Language group. She was totally uncommunicative. She did not want to join in the PE lessons. The apparatus in the hall simply terrified her. On the computer she spent a great deal of the time either doodling on the screen or just playing with the keys. Gradually this gave way to more structured work, with the result that she became more open to direction and suggestions from me and the other children. Finally after what seemed to be endless sessions of messing about, Jasmin began to make up her own programs.

Last week in the PE class she leapt off the box and went into a forward roll. I think she was more surprised than we were. Jasmin has also begun to sing and is now determined to participate in class activities.

Sharif (nine years old) also comes from Pakistan. He speaks good English. A few days ago he made a significant breakthrough in Maths. After much experimenting at the keyboard, he managed to teach the computer to draw a circle. At the beginning of the first term with me, he spent most of the time annoying the other children. He was argumentative and at times very disruptive.

Over the weeks he has taught the computer to execute many of his programs. His energy is now directly channelled into his work, not only on the computer, but also in his story-writing and other subjects of the first school curriculum. Sharif is totally absorbed in his computer projects and has given up being a nuisance to others. On the contrary, his lively mind is an asset to the general motivation of the class as a whole.

You may think that I have been describing exceptional children in an idyllic teaching situation. This is not so. My work has been done with an average inner city class of eight and nine year olds. The children's view of the world is in fact rather limited. They spend most of their leisure time watching television or playing on the streets. Some of the children play with electronic games; some own calculators and are familiar with micros, at least in the sense that they have seen them on television and in the shops.

In general the expectations of the school do not correspond to the children's limited experience of life. Children appear to be lacking in self-motivation. But are they? Could it not be that school and the pressure that it imposes on its charges are unrelated to the private life of the child?

Does a gulf exist between what the school expects from the children and what the children themselves understand? I believe that such a gulf does exist. Furthermore I believe that the microcomputer is able to bridge this gulf. The micro enables someone like Leon, for example, to develop his potential and creativity within the school situation. Much depends on how the computer is used. Primarily the micro allows the individual child to explore and make learning a personal venture. There is no need to keep up with your brighter classmates. You do not rush to finish Book Two in order to start Book Three, since knowledge is personal and learning takes place at your own pace. I do not consider the use of textbooks in computer education to be irrelevant, but I do want to stress the importance of active learning — using books as opposed to being enslaved by them. I support a selective approach to learning by which the child is not dependent on factual learning, but is in command and can ask questions.

School places a high value on abstract thinking, which in turn is reflected in our understanding of academic success. The more proficient we are at abstract thinking, say for example using algebraic symbols or simply using adult language, the more we are likely to succeed in the educational system.

Unfortunately it requires a considerable leap from the child's own reasoning, based on the familiar and the everyday, to the abstract or formal thinking that is demanded in the classroom. Here the micro can also help. It can provide a concrete approach to the abstract concepts of mathematics, for example, or can enable the children to interact with the computer via story-writing and true-life situations, known as simulations.

Our use of the micro in school began with LOGO, using the graphics facilities of the computer to draw on the screen. No pressure or demands were made on the children. They were shown a few basic drawing commands and then left to explore the endless possibilities of screen doodling. Only when the children were ready, did I ask them to draw me something specific. Only when they had explored at the level they understood and with which they could identify, did I suggest that they draw familiar shapes such as a square, an oblong or a triangle.

Sharif, Jasmin, Leon and the others in the class found themselves becoming personally involved in their work. They were beginning to realise that they were free to explore at their own level of understanding without me as the teacher telling them what to do all the time. That does not mean that they were free from any form of direction, but rather that their work on the computer was self-motivated.

Sean suddenly announced that he had better get down to learning his nine times table. He wanted to draw a pattern using right angles and needed to know how to calculate 90, 180, 270, and 360 degrees. He had discovered a relationship between these particular angles and the products or multiples of nine. Incidentally Sean is way behind in traditional school Maths.

Are these children exceptions? In my opinion, yes — if you passionately believe that all children are! Perhaps it is better to ask whether these children represent the norm found in most schools. I still say yes, and I think many teachers would agree. The problem is to find the best means by which to communicate with our children; to present lessons, projects, topics and all areas of the curriculum in such a way that children like Sean or Jasmin respond in a positive way, making that knowledge part and parcel of their own experience.

Has the presence of the micro in the classroom played a part in developing a positive attitude towards learning? Has LOGO helped to reveal a hidden intelligence, which our school system has failed to notice?

I believe that LOGO was instrumental in revealing the hidden potential of such children as Leon, Jasmin, Sharif and the other microchildren in my class. How did it do this? LOGO did this by providing a stimulating environment for learning, through practical activities at the level of each child's understanding. It liberated their attitude towards learning. It was meaningful and fulfilling.

I would like to share my own experiences of using LOGO with young children and invite you to join me on a journey into a fascinating world of creativity and problem-solving. The only prerequisite you need is a willingness to learn alongside your children.

Although LOGO is not a rigid programming language, it is highly structured. Children begin by learning simple commands, which can be combined to form simple procedures. Simple procedures in turn can be used as commands to build more complex procedures and so on. As the child works with the basic tools of LOGO, whole new worlds in geometry and language development are opened up. Furthermore the learning is open-ended. There are no set goals to achieve, in the formal sense, since LOGO offers exploration and learning at the child's own pace. LOGO is also a way of thinking through programming. The developers of LOGO were in fact concerned with the study of intelligence and how children develop intellectually. Based on contemporary ideas in educational psychology, a parallel was drawn between intellectual development and methods of computation. The study of intelligence was expressed by means of computer programs, which gave rise to the notion that the way we think could be linked to a particular style of programming. The result was LOGO. LOGO is therefore an introduction both to computing and to thinking.

My immediate concern is young children in the first school, but that does not mean that the ideas in this book cannot be used in the secondary school, or by adults for that matter. Part 4 of this book (LOGO Workshop) introduces you to some advanced ideas, which young children will certainly not be able to produce themselves. They are included as a guide or a tool to the endless possibilities offered by LOGO.

2 Which Micro? Which Language?

What is a Micro?

Without going into technical details, which are beyond the scope of this book, for our purposes the microcomputer is nothing more than a tool. It is a tool that can handle or process information at great speed. In the 1970s, the micro-processor chip changed the basis of computing by reducing the computer from a machine that filled a whole room to one that could fit into a suitcase. Suddenly the computer was not just available to business and industry, but to schools as well. A subsequent fall in the price of microcomputers, combined with the development of the software industry, has produced a rapid growth in the number and types of microcomputer available at this time.

Data storage and retrieval
Information is usually fed into the computer via a typewriter keyboard, *?!* although there are other input-devices such as probes, speech synthesisers and TV cameras etc., depending on usage. The computer outputs information usually by means of a screen monitor or printer. Information or data, as it is generally called in computing, can also be stored in the computer's memory. This information can be stored permanently in its ROM (read-only memory), where it remains unchanged, or in its RAM (random-access memory), to which you have access should you wish to change the information. The amount of RAM in your computer is decisive in how much memory you can use. A word of warn- ing here. Although some micros on the market claim to provide plenty of RAM, not all of this is available to the user. Always check on how much RAM you can actually use.

The micro is a machine that processes information that is put into it. Generally speaking, if you input incorrect data, the micro will obligingly output the incorrect data. This is known in computer circles as the GIGO Principle — Garbage in; Garbage out. Whether it is used for the purpose of calculating the square root of 99 or for balancing the household bills, you the user must be able to communicate with the computer. The computer itself works by using a series of electrical impulses. These in turn have to be decoded and translated into *strange idea* normal or nearly normal language (a high level language), which the user can *of direction!* understand. These electrical impulses can also be represented arithmetically as a sequence of ones and zeros, known as machine code (low level language). It is however very taxing for a person to try and work with machine code and therefore the development of high level languages has made it easier for the user. Even so, extreme accuracy is needed whatever language you use. I have spent many gruelling hours working with a modified machine code. As an intelligence analyst I was engaged in converting intelligence code into computer code. This required a great deal of accuracy. A comma left out or a figure misplaced would produce garbled nonsense. It was reported that one of the NASA space flights was aborted because of a missing hyphen in the launching program — a typing error that cost the US Government billions of dollars!

Which Micro?

Choosing a micro for your children at home or at school needs careful consideration. Of all the micros available commercially, and there are many, only a few are suitable for educational purposes. How do you assess a computer's educational suitability? I would propose the following criteria.

1. The micro should, apart from BASIC, be able to run several other languages, especially LOGO, PROLOG and LISP.
2. It should have a good range of quality software, which is readily available.
3. It should be backed up by reliable servicing at a reasonable price.
4. It should have high resolution graphics, colour and sound. A music facility is especially important for schools.

There are at least five machines that immediately fulfil these criteria. They are the TANDY COLOR computer, the APPLE II, the Sinclair SPECTRUM, the Research Machine 380Z, and the BBC Model B. Unfortunately the APPLE and the RML 380Z are expensive machines and most schools that would benefit from one or more of these computers do not have sufficient funds to acquire them. Price-wise the BBC stands midway, while the TANDY and the SPECTRUM are cheaper, being well within the price range of the buyer who wants to use them in the home or primary school. What all these machines have in common is the first criterion, and in particular LOGO (although this is not yet available for the BBC Model B).

Which Language?

Programming in BASIC

The main language associated with these five micros and with most personal micros is BASIC (Beginners All-purpose Symbolic Instruction Code). This was designed for beginners, as the name suggests, and is fairly easy to learn. BASIC uses English words and phrases such as PRINT, LET, and IF . . . THEN. There are many more and the number of words depends on the version of BASIC that you use. I have found that six-year-olds can write elementary programs to perform simple addition and subtraction. Easy problems are indeed easy to solve. However, if you try to write more sophisticated programs, or attempt to solve difficult problems, you run into trouble. If, like many older children, you wish to write your own computer games or, like many teachers, to write your own software for the classroom, you soon discover how complicated and time-consuming programming in BASIC is.

A complex language

To write a good program using graphics and sound effects requires a great deal of time and mental effort, juggling with such things as sub-routines, loops, and GOTOs. You find yourself plodding through a maze of complicated statements. A glance through any of the computer magazines on sale at your local news-agents will reveal lengthy pages of complicated games' programs, which you can copy into your machine.

This is not to say that BASIC is of no value whatsoever, but rather that its importance has been greatly exaggerated. I would also question its role in computer education. Some very good programs are written in BASIC. I use several myself in the classroom and at home. They have nevertheless been written by professional software writers and could not easily be undertaken by children, or by teachers for that matter, since the writing of such programs is a full-time occupation.

The simple fact is that BASIC is not as basic as it would appear. Despite the fact that there are some structured BASICS, such as BBC BASIC which uses procedures, BASIC still appears rather clumsy and cumbersome in the light of more recent languages. Is the relationship of BASIC to programming what valves were to computers? To use micro-jargon, BASIC is more machine friendly than user friendly. In other words it was written for the micro rather than for the non-technical user. It may be that the commercial manufacturers of personal computers decided that, since BASIC was relatively cheap to produce (it requires very little memory, usually 8 K as compared with the 64 K used by other languages), it was a viable language on the consumer market.

It is unfortunate that schools and colleges still persist in teaching BASIC as the main computer language. Already micros are becoming powerful enough to support systems that are designed for the convenience of people rather than machines. We need to break away from the micro-cult with its emphasis on programming for its own sake and realise that programming is a means of describing things. The micro is a powerful tool, which can open up a vast source of ideas, not only in science, but also in all areas of knowledge.

Programming with logic

A step in this direction is a new high level language known as PROLOG (PROgramming with LOGic). Developed by Dr Robert Kowalski at Imperial College, London, it has been used experimentally in some schools. Although it is not strictly a programming language for children, it is beginning to gain ground in some classrooms, in the form of Micro-PROLOG, a version especially developed for schools.

Expert systems

PROLOG is useful in producing expert systems. Expert or specialist knowledge is stored in the computer. This in turn is processed according to the rules of the subject, be it history, geography, or science, with the result that the computer comes up with logical conclusions about what it has digested. A doctor, for example, could store his expert knowledge of disease, symptoms and current drugs in the computer's memory, in the form of PROLOG data. If he has a problem case, he can refer to the computer and feed in the patient's symptoms and ask the machine to scan its data and find anything relevant. The computer searches the data and will produce not only the diseases where these symptoms are obvious, but also the diseases where any of these symptoms occur. The final judgement, however, is made by the doctor and not by the machine. The computer can also ask the doctor for additional data, such as blood pressure or pulse.

In the classroom the children ask the micro relevant questions about the subject that they are investigating, while the computer produces logical conclusions. It also asks the children appropriate questions, the answers to which help to fill in any missing information.

Although children can write quite sophisticated programs in Micro-PROLOG, its real value is intelligent interaction with the computer. If you know the right questions to ask, then you probably have a good understanding of what you are learning. The value of Micro-PROLOG has however not yet been fully assessed. It is still in an experimental stage, although a version is already available for the Sinclair SPECTRUM. Micro-PROLOG can be used as a database for most subjects of the curriculum. It has already been used successfully in History, French and English Language. What Micro-PROLOG cannot offer is computer experience for young children.

LOGO programming

In contrast to this, LOGO is a very powerful computer language, which like natural language, can be learnt by the youngest child. It is not however an alternative to Micro-PROLOG. LOGO is a different approach to learning.

LOGO began in the 1960s under the inspiration of Seymour Papert, an educationalist and computer scientist working at the Massachusetts Institute of Technology (MIT).

Papert developed a computer language for children, which combined the ideas of the Swiss psychologist Jean Piaget and those of the Artificial Intelligence researchers at MIT with whom he was associated. Papert, like Piaget, saw children as active builders of their knowledge rather than passive learners of facts. Could very young children learn to program and play with computers in their learning? Could they use the computer within a creative context, so that they became thinkers? Papert believed they could. He talked not only about LOGO as a computer language but as a philosophy of education.

The essence of LOGO is that even pre-school children can teach the computer new words and routines (called procedures), in any way they wish, using very simple commands. Learning in LOGO does not depend on an outside agent but is initiated by the learner — the child himself.

A language for everyone

LOGO has also been specifically designed to make its use easy, but at the same time it allows you to explore the language to any depth or level of sophistication that you wish. You can, by using turtle graphics, draw simple shapes or explore Newtonian physics with the dynaturtle. You can play with patterns in the nursery or investigate the Theory of Relativity at university level. You can discover such profound mathematical ideas as variable stepping and recursion, or simply doodle on the screen for pleasure. LOGO can also be used to write quiz programs or to create a databank for storing and manipulating words and lists. LOGO is not just mathematics, its list processing facility can be applied to language in general. But perhaps most important of all, LOGO allows you to invent your own personal programs. It enables you to make up your own language for use on the computer.

LOGO also familiarises young children with many areas of modern mathematics. A two-year-old can guide the floor turtle around objects or make it draw lines on the floor, while at the same time learning intuitively about differential calculus and topology. Derived from LISP, the language of Artificial Intelligence, LOGO allows infants to play with the ideas of advanced computer science.

Real LOGO

Like real ale, real LOGO is powerful stuff. It should not be confused with a watered-down substitute that is known as turtle graphics. With an ever-growing interest in LOGO, several turtle graphics programs have appeared. Some of these are pseudo-LOGOs and, since they are not representative of real LOGO, they should be avoided. They tend to undermine the power and potential of real LOGO, and certainly do not demonstrate that LOGO is a valuable tool for thinking. These inferior substitutes actually make programming more difficult. They do not have the essential features of LOGO, which are:

1. Recursion.
2. User-defined names for variables. Children should be able to build up their own vocabulary.
3. Local variables. It is essential that variables are local to procedures in which they are defined.
4. Screen-editing. Children must be able to see and edit their procedures.
5. A top-down facility. This style of programming is central to LOGO. Children must be encouraged to take a large problem and reduce it into smaller manageable parts which they can test individually.

A LOGO without these features is not LOGO. You can usually recognise pseudo-LOGOs by their titles. These usually masquerade under such brand names as LOGO Challenge or FORTH LOGO.

Critics of real LOGO say that it is kids' stuff. It is! Kids bright or mentally retarded, autistic or physically handicapped, have used LOGO intelligently, and have at the same time been able to demonstrate a creativity and feeling for mathematical thinking that has not been previously recorded.

3 Use and Misuse of the Micro

LOGO is a rich and versatile language which is beginning to make its way into education. Like any new idea its implementation in schools has been rather slow. There are two major reasons for this. The first is an economic one. Full implementations of LOGO are only available on expensive machines, such as the APPLE II and RML 380Z. One machine per school is simply not enough. Even cheaper computers like the TANDY COLOR or Sinclair SPECTRUM are still too expensive for the average primary school, where the requirement is for at least two computers per class of approximately 28 children. The second and more influential reason is an in-built resistance by traditional schooling to LOGO philosophy, and in particular to LOGO maths. Even some protagonists of LOGO are not willing to implement Papert's philosophy, regarding it as too utopian and radical for their liking. Despite the advances in technology and science, schools in general still persist in teaching Victorian arithmetic. Although we live in the latter part of the twentieth century, the mathematics curriculum in the UK is still based on the Education Code of the 1860s.

At the beginning of this century, there was a premium for being good at mani-pulating figures, without necessarily being able to interpret the results. Ledger clerks skilled in arithmetic could readily find a job. Today however it is different. It is the person who can understand mathematics who is more likely to succeed in the future, rather than one who can only carry out arithmetical operations, however efficiently and skilfully. This is not to say that arithmetic or, to be more precise, the basic skills of addition, subtraction, multiplication and division, are not fundamental to our understanding of number. It is the approach or method that needs reconsideration.

In the 1960s we saw the introduction of the New Maths, consisting of sets, functions, topology and other ideas taken directly from university courses. These subjects were simplified and then introduced into the infant classroom. The old content of the mathematics curriculum did in fact begin to give way to the modern maths. However the old methods continued.

At the same time as the New Maths was being introduced, a whole range of teaching machines appeared. These consisted of programmed texts and large mechanical monsters that put the children through their paces, or at least tried, since much of this equipment spent a great part of its life in the repair shop. Although a considerable amount of energy and money was spent on their development, these machines died a quick death. The remains of some still lurk today in dusty cupboards. They now seem like the dinosaurs of old, relics of an enthusiastic but misguided philosophy of education.

The advent of the micro into schools was followed by computer aided learning (CAL). This, despite its attractive packaging, is all too often drill and practice learning. The computer is used as an exerciser and tutor. The child is regarded as a machine, to be programmed and conditioned by the computer. The creators of this type of learning are known as behavioural psychologists. Most of their work has been carried out on pigeons and white rats. They see effective learning as a form of conditioning. Like the first motor car, the micro (as one journalist put it) is often seen in terms of a horseless carriage. As petrol was considered to be a replacement for hay, so the computer is used as a substitute for pencil and paper. This is a blatant example of twentieth century technology reinforcing nineteenth century practices.

Although conditioning does have its place in some areas of learning, such as foreign languages or the teaching of mechanical skills, in mathematics it is anathema. Children sitting in front of screens, passively learning facts presented to them via CAL, are reminiscent of the Victorian classroom with its rows of desks. Some children learn by this method, but do they become thinkers?

Today's world needs thinkers, designers, and decision-makers, not operators, however proficient and dedicated they may be. You will probably have met the student with the photographic memory, who can digest reams of information and successfully pass examinations, without making this acquired knowledge part of his or her own wisdom. There is some use for CAL in the classroom, but it is limited.

The question you must ask yourself as a parent is – do I want my child to be a programmer or to be programmed? Which is your child – an operator or a thinker? It is good that children should learn the skills of number and language, the tricks of the trade so to speak, but surely not at the expense of understanding and enjoying number? We all need to learn skills, but not at the expense of creative thinking.

Is BASIC Bad for You?

In some schools, there is an unhealthy emphasis on skills, especially in computer studies. The skill of programming can become an end in itself. This has in some extreme cases produced what psychiatrists are calling micro-addiction or compulsive programming. The computer becomes an obsession. Some children faced with the complexity of BASIC, for example, become totally engrossed in the programming. They tend to forget the outside world and have been known to find the micro more friendly and more understanding than their classmates. BASIC may not cause the phenomenon of compulsive programming, but it may

why BASIC ?

facilitate it. For many teachers and computer enthusiasts in general, BASIC means programming. It is for them what computing is all about. It is *the* language supplied with most micros. *So what?*

Compulsive programming is a serious problem in some North American universities, where micro-addicts live, eat and frequently sleep at the keyboard. Young micro-addicts prefer to talk to computers rather than people. At home they are mistakenly taken for computer geniuses by doting parents, who encourage them to sit for hours in front of the screen, sometimes until the early hours of the morning, in order to get a program just right. Compulsive programming is like using a spade for digging the garden, without ever planting anything. The digging turns out to be such an obsessive activity that it eventually becomes both the means and the end. This addiction to the micro may be one of the factors that adds to the mystique that surrounds it. I wish to dispel this mystique by stating that the micro is a machine and nothing more. It is simply a tool that we can use in either a positive or negative way. Using PROLOG or LOGO in school or home creates an attitude towards computing that is functional and creative. The computer is a tool to be used in all areas of the curriculum. The role of LOGO in school has already been described, but perhaps its emphasis on personalised learning needs to be re-affirmed. This is not the case with BASIC. The very nature of this language tends towards the phenomenon of programming for its own sake. The complexity of BASIC and the need to perform acrobatic *why ??* manipulations of the language to produce clever programs made one critic call it BASIC spaghetti.

4 Procedural Thinking

Many children become competent in the basic skills of arithmetic, but when it is a question of problem-solving they seem unable to use these skills. Taps filling baths or men mowing meadows, these types of problem seem very remote from the child's experience. How are Leon and Jasmin to relate to such abstract problems in the classroom? How can children use the skills that they have mastered in the real world?

Two members of the class, Kate and Wendy, are drawing a house on the screen. Kate begins by drawing a square. She is pleased with this, but stops to consider how to draw a roof.

Wendy: 'You'll need a triangle. Just put it on top.'
Kate: 'Then we can put in windows and a door.'

Kate starts drawing a triangle. Her first attempt does not work. Her second attempt produces a triangle but she cannot make it fit on top of the square.

Kate: 'What shall we do now?'
Wendy: 'I don't know — it won't fit. Ask Mr Gascoigne.'
Me. 'What's the problem Kate?'
Wendy: 'We can't get the roof on.'
Me: 'Have you tried drawing a triangle on its own?'
Kate: 'Yes, but you have a go Wendy.'

Wendy clears the screen and proceeds to draw a triangle. It does not work.

Me: 'You know how to draw a square. What is the procedure?'

Wendy goes through the procedure for a square as follows

```
Forward 50 Right 90 Forward 50 Right 90

Forward 50 Right 90 Forward 50 Right 90
```

Me: 'How many forwards do you need to draw a triangle?'
Wendy: 'Three!'
Me: 'How do you turn?'
Kate: '90?'
Me: 'Well try and see what happens. If that does not work, try a different input.'

5 minutes later

Kate: 'We still can't do it.'
Wendy: 'We can't get the line to join up.'

This conversation took place only a few days after the introduction of the micro into the class. Kate and Wendy had quickly passed from doodling and drawing by trial and error towards procedural thinking. Wendy knew that to draw a house you could start with the procedure for a square or for an oblong, depending on what type of house you wanted. They both knew that they needed a triangle for the roof, but could not work out a procedure for drawing one that would fit.

Sean (six weeks later) is trying to write a procedure to draw a spaceship. He uses a triangle and a square procedure that he has written previously. He now has to join his triangle and square to make the fuselage and nose cone of the spaceship. Sean knows what he wants his picture to look like and requires very little outside help.

However as he proceeds to draw two boosters for the spaceship, he makes his first error. He does not use a procedure to construct the boosters. Instead of writing one procedure to draw a small triangle and using it twice, he draws the boosters by a trial and error method of moving the turtle around the screen. Time and time again the screen turtle crashes into the side of the fuselage, but to no avail. The result of each attack does not resemble a booster. What is to be done? As Sean works he thinks aloud. He shifts about in his chair, twisting his body as he tries to work out the movements of the turtle. 'This is hard work!' he exclaims.

Sean does not use pencil and paper like some of the other children, but prefers to work out his ideas in his head. He eventually realises that he needs to calculate the correct angle. His efforts produce a systematic procedure for the boosters, which he calls Smalltri. His spaceship now needs a window. He remembers drawing polygons previously and chooses to design a hexagonal window.

LOGO in this type of situation permits the child to tackle a problem by reducing it to mind-sized bits. Sean in this case takes something new, the procedure spaceship, and relates it to what he already knows — the procedures for square, triangle etc. Procedural thinking teaches him about his own thinking. It provides him with a method of organising his thoughts and ideas. Without this systematical approach, Sean, Kate and Wendy are forced to approach problems in a groping, abstract fashion. Furthermore, learning to build with smaller structures within a system makes it possible in the long run for the child to grasp the system as a whole. Conversely, being able to reduce a problem into smaller structures is a very useful skill. In LOGO it is known as topping-down. Given time and experience, children like Kate and Wendy should be able to look at a fairly complex pattern and be able to write a program to reproduce it, by reducing the pattern down to its basic building procedures.

Have you got a Bug?

An integral part of any problem-solving strategy is dealing with mistakes as they
arise. Kate and Wendy's roof had a mistake in the procedure, which they
recognised but could not correct. Mistakes, or bugs as they are called in programming, are in some ways essential to organised thinking. How many times do we
hear the cry 'I can't do that!' or 'We haven't done that before!'? Children learning LOGO come to accept mistakes or bugs in their programming. Instead of the
negative attitude of regarding themselves as failures if things go wrong, they
learn to accept the fact that they have a bug somewhere in their thinking. In
extreme circumstances they can blame the computer!

What does that feel like?

   Debugging is therefore fundamental to good, effective learning. It is also
fundamental to procedural thinking. Children do not get despondent or readily
give up if they cannot solve problems immediately. The maxim is: if it doesn't
work, then find the bug! No-one can in fact write a bug-free program. No-one
of course can avoid errors. Children have to be made aware of this. Life is not
just one success after another. The sooner children learn that bugs are part and
parcel of learning, the sooner they will gain self-confidence and, above all, the
ability to have a go at all that comes their way.
   Procedural thinking is not only applicable to Turtle Geometry, but can also
be applied across the school curriculum. George is having trouble in Gym Club,
trying to learn a backward roll. At my suggestion he approaches this by procedural thinking. Together we break down the procedure for the backward roll
into individual movements and think about where he goes wrong. First you
crouch down with arms stretched out in front. You then tuck in your head and
roll backwards, lifting your legs as you move, etc. Like magic, after several
attempts he manages to perform a backward roll — well, after a fashion! Mind
over matter, I think to myself.
   Nearly everything we do is governed by procedures although we do not
necessarily think about the method but rather the end product. Driving a car,
for example, is a procedure. Daily procedures like getting dressed become
habitual, they are second nature to us. What about problem-solving? Can we
use our procedural thinking to fix the car? There are two approaches to car
maintenance. The first is to look under the bonnet and close it quickly in
dismay. The second is to reach for the handbook and systematically check
through the procedures for fault-finding. You might at this point raise the
objection that some people have a knack for certain things and I would not
deny this. If on the other hand we viewed learning procedurally, we might
achieve more. 'I can't draw. I can't do Maths. I was never good at science.'
Perhaps if we had asked ourselves 'Where's the bug in my understanding or
attitude?' then we might have found a hidden talent, albeit a tiny one, in some
areas of knowledge which we shy away from as adults.

PART 2: LOGO LEARNING — TURTLE GEOMETRY

5 How to Teach Your Child

When children first meet the computer, they should be allowed to play. Although it may look to you like messing about, it isn't. Play is the child's way of exploring and coming to terms with what is new. Of course play is not restricted to children alone. Scientists, engineers, artists, in fact all of us, play. We explore and investigate in order to find out how things work. If I am stating the obvious I beg your indulgence. There is nevertheless a tendency sometimes for adults to overlook this essential and vital activity of children. You must at all costs avoid interfering in the initial stages of LOGO learning. Better still, have a go yourself. Place yourself in the situation of the young learner. Let children see that you too are a beginner, an explorer like them. Your ideas and experience should complement your child's learning, not replace it. On no account should you formalise the learning. The first encounter with LOGO should therefore consist of play. Very young children should be allowed to play with the keyboard if they want to, before drawing on the screen. You can of course cover up the keys that you do not want the children to use, by means of a piece of stiff card. (My three-year-old daughter Xenia watched me many times working at the keyboard, but when it came to her turn she was more interested in typing her 'X' as she called it, rather than moving the turtle.)

How to Begin

There are four basic commands in LOGO (figure 1)

```
FORWARD

BACKWARD

RIGHT

LEFT
```

These can be abbreviated to FD, BK, RT, and LT, depending on which micro you use. (Commands used here are for TANDY LOGO and TERRAPIN LOGO.)

21

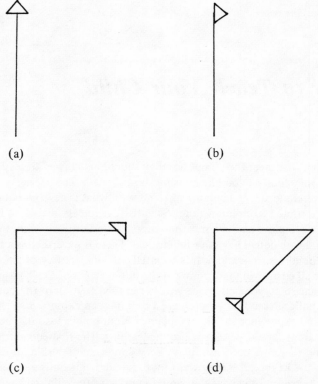

Figure 1: (a) FD 100; (b) RT 90; (c) FD 80 LT 45; (d) BK 90

The screen turtle (or floor turtle) needs an input number, to tell it how many steps to move or how many degrees to turn.

FORWARD 10	RIGHT 90
BACKWARD 20	LEFT 180

Typing FORWARD 10 and pressing the RETURN/ENTER key (or equivalent) will move the turtle ten paces forward. As the turtle moves it draws a line. If you wish to turn the turtle, type RIGHT or LEFT, followed by the number of degrees you wish it to turn. RIGHT 90, for example, will turn the turtle 90 degrees to the right. (Do not forget to press RETURN after each command.) The micro also likes you to leave a space between FORWARD and 10. If you forget, an error message will appear on the screen. Each LOGO normally has its own syntax rules and you should consult the particular user-manual for your machine. All micros are nonetheless very particular and will respond only to correct commands. Children soon learn that precision and logic are essential if they wish to obtain the required results. ("Oh no! I forgot to press the space bar!") What might seem pernickety and pedantic to adults is accepted without question by young programmers. Simply working with the micro teaches the children to be precise and logical in their thinking. Before looking at the following examples, try some commands yourself and see what happens.

Example 1
At the keyboard

	Effect on the screen
FORWARD 100	Turtle moves forward 100 steps
RIGHT 45	Turtle rotates 45 degrees to the right
FORWARD 50	Turtle moves forward 50 steps
LEFT 70	Turtle rotates 70 degrees to the left
BACKWARD 200	Turtle moves backward 200 steps

You can also move the turtle without drawing a line. To do this type PENUP or PU. The opposite of this command is PENDOWN or PD.

PU	Turtle lifts the pen
FD 75	Moves forward 75 steps
PD	Turtle lowers the pen
BK 8	Moves backward 8 steps

Example 2
A dotted line (figure 2)

Figure 2: A dotted line

FD 10	PU
PU	FD 10
FD 10	PD
PD	FD 10..........
FD 10	

Using Single Keys with Pre-school Children and Infants

There are various implementations of LOGO that use single keys to operate the turtle.

OK LOGO — for use with the JESSOP Floor Turtle
One-Key LOGO uses the following keys

F	— Forward	D	— Pendown
B	— Backward	U	— Penup
R	— Right	H	— Plays a tune
L	— Left		

I found it useful to cover up the other keys by using a piece of card, leaving only the seven basic command keys and the numerical keys exposed. Separate keyboards are also available with extra large buttons. They have been successfully used with physically handicapped children in the USA.

INSTANT COMMAND used with TERRAPIN LOGO
This is a do-it-yourself LOGO. You type in your own commands. It is particularly useful if you wish to use other keys later. You do not need to be an experienced programmer to do this.

Type the following

```
TO INSTANT

COMMAND

INSTANT

END
```

This sets up the procedure for the one-key response. Now type

```
TO COMMAND

MAKE "COMM READCHARACTER

IF :COMM = "F FORWARD 10

IF :COMM = "R RIGHT 30

IF :COMM = "L LEFT 30

IF :COMM = "B BACKWARD 10

END
```

At a later stage you might like to add

```
IF :COMM = "X PENUP

IF :COMM = "Y PENDOWN
```

You can also use other keys for other commands or even procedures (provided that you have defined them) such that the S key draws a square or T draws a triangle. Just define what you want them to do and include them in the procedure COMMAND.

TANDY OK LOGO

TANDY also has a One-Key facility similar to that of TERRAPIN. Any key can be defined for this purpose. Children can move the turtle around the screen using the number keys and can produce triangles by pressing T, squares by pressing S, circles by pressing C, or whatever shape you have defined.

My favourite is the TANDY DOODLE Mode. A plastic overlay with symbols is fitted over the top row of the keyboard. These symbols on the overlay correspond to the number keys, but change their functions: (1) becomes − clear the screen; (2) − home turtle; (3) − PENUP; (4) − PENDOWN; (5) − RT 45; (6) − LT 45; (7) − FD 1; (8) − FD 10; (9) − RT 15; (0) − LT 15.

Further details of these systems are fully discussed in the appropriate user-manual.

6 Using Simple Commands

Having doodled and drawn simple shapes manually at the keyboard, you are now ready to teach the micro to do this. You begin by typing the word TO. This tells the computer that you are going to teach it something. (In TANDY LOGO you have to enter the edit mode to do this.) You can now put the basic commands (FD, BK, RT and LT) together to make a program or procedure. Say for example you wish to draw a square, then you would type TO SQUARE or, as I tell my children, use your own name. The statement TO sets up the computer and the word SQUARE executes it. A typical procedure should look something like the following

TO SQUARE	TO SEAN
FD 100	FD 100
RT 90	RT 90
FD 100	FD 100
RT 90	RT 90
FD 100	FD 100
RT 90	RT 90
FD 100	FD 100
END	END

Not state transparent.
(P30)

Both procedures will tell the computer to draw a square (figure 3). TO SEAN or TO WENDY has of course more personal meaning and is in fact the mere beginning of the greater things to come. We are entering the world of personalised knowledge, a micro-world where you create your own language and ideas. This is just the tip of the iceberg of personal learning — but more of that later.

It is again important to allow the children to play, to experiment with the TO statement. It is important that they should be left alone to explore and enjoy the power and satisfaction of teaching the computer new tricks. It will not be long before you are bombarded with questions such as 'How can I make the turtle draw several squares', or 'How do you write a procedure for a triangle', etc. Resist any inner urge to demonstrate if your child or group of children do

26

Figure 3: SQUARE

not ask questions! Unless they are seriously limited in imagination, it does not take long for the questions to flow and for you to be dragged into their arguments about which is the best procedure to use.

Whenever you write a procedure using the TO statement, the computer stores it in its memory. It becomes a part of the computer's vocabulary. Every time you type the word that you have defined, either SQUARE or SEAN or whatever, the turtle will draw the appropriate shape. The micro now understands SQUARE in the same way that it understands LT, RT, FD and BK.

The following are examples of the use of the TO statement (figures 4, 5 and 6)

TO TRIANGLE	TO OBLONG	TO DIAMOND
FD 40	FD 55	FD 50
LT 120	RT 90	RT 45
FD 40	FD 30	FD 50
LT 120	RT 90	RT 135
FD 40	FD 55	FD 50
LT 120	RT 90	RT 45
END	FD 30	FD 50
	END	END

Figure 4: TRIANGLE   *Figure 5: OBLONG*   *Figure 6: DIAMOND*

Typing each individual command is rather laborious, especially if you have written a lengthy procedure. To overcome this you can use the word REPEAT. Thus instead of writing a long list of commands you can write

```
TO OBLONG

REPEAT 2 (FD 55 RT 90 FD 30 RT 90)

END
```

The commands FD 55 and FD 30 together with the angle RT 90 are repeated twice. They are placed in parentheses for this reason.

```
TO TRIANGLE                    TO SQUARE

REPEAT 3 (FD 40 RT 120)        REPEAT 4 (FD 100 RT 90)

END                            END
```

Perhaps you can guess which shape the next procedure will produce

```
TO ?

REPEAT 36 (FD 10 RT 10)

END
```

It is again important that children should be given the opportunity to experiment with the statement REPEAT. Here are some further ideas for repetition.

First type   *Now type*
```
TO ARC                         TO ARC1

FD 20 RT 20                     REPEAT 10 (FD 20 RT 20)

FD 20 RT 20                     END

END
```

```
TO ?

REPEAT 10 (REPEAT 4 (FD 50 RT 90) RT 36)

END
```

Copy this very carefully and do not forget to include all the parentheses listed. If this procedure does not work, then you have a bug somewhere. It could be that you forgot to include all the parentheses or that you forgot the spacing between commands and inputs. As I said before, bugs and the process of debugging are part and parcel of normal programming. Perhaps now you would like to test the limits of your machine by thinking up a procedure that uses repeats of repeats *ad infinitum.* When Kate first sat at the keyboard she insisted on giving the micro impossible inputs until she was satisfied that the computer was only a 'dumb' machine after all.

LOGO Primitives and Procedures

So far I have introduced you to the command words FORWARD, BACKWARD, LEFT, RIGHT, PENUP, PENDOWN and the control statements TO and REPEAT. These LOGO words belong to the internal vocabulary of the computer and are known as primitives. There are many more and we shall meet them later.

Other command words such as SQUARE, TRIANGLE, SEAN or WENDY are called procedures. These are the commands that you teach the computer. Whenever you create a new procedure it is automatically added to the micro's vocabulary. Children can therefore construct their own language for use with the computer. The significance of this 'teaching' of the computer is considerable, especially in terms of creative learning.

7 Sub-procedures

A procedure can call or use other procedures as a part of its program. An example of this is the procedure JASMIN (figure 7)

✗ See p 26

```
TO JASMIN

SQUARE

SQUARE

SQUARE

SQUARE

END
```

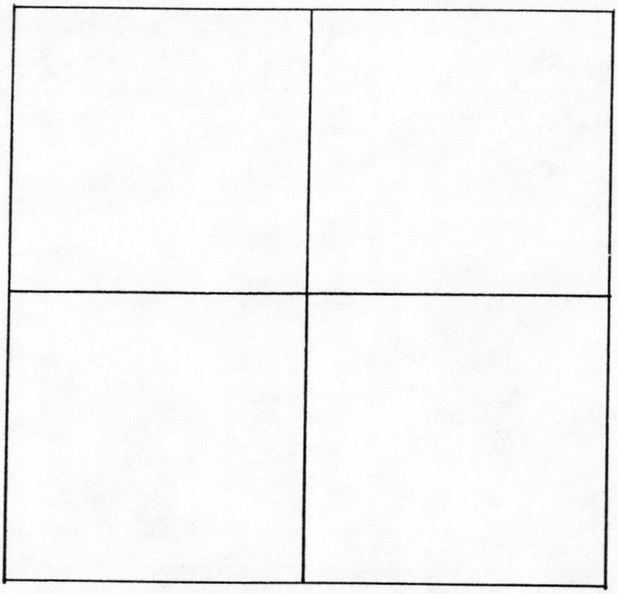

Figure 7: JASMIN

JASMIN is the name of the program or procedure. Here the real live Jasmin used the procedure SQUARE (she had written previously) four times. She used SQUARE as a sub-procedure within the new procedure that she called JASMIN.

Let us look at her procedure called SQUARE.

```
TO SQUARE

FD 100

RT 90

FD 100

RT 90

FD 100

RT 90

FD 100

END
```

SQUARE was then repeated four times.

Once JASMIN had discovered sub-procedures, things really took off! She later went on to use JASMIN as a sub-procedure of JASMIN. This is known in mathematics as recursion (see chapter 8).

You can take any procedure and use it as a sub-procedure for another program. Thus the procedure BOX can be used as a sub-procedure of a new procedure — let us call it FOUR. FOUR in its turn can be called or used as a sub-procedure of MANY (figure 8)

```
TO BOX

FD 50 RT 90

FD 30 RT 90

FD 50 RT 90

FD 30

END
```

```
TO FOUR                TO MANY

REPEAT 4 (BOX)         REPEAT 5 (FOUR RT 18)

END                    END
```

Figure 8: MANY

The Top-down Method

So far you have used procedures like building blocks to create new procedures.
You have defined a first procedure, then written a second procedure that used
the first procedure as a sub-procedure etc. The emphasis has been on the
mechanics of LOGO rather than on problem-solving. One of the important

Figure 9: PATTERN

features of LOGO however is the top-down method of programming. You
should start with an idea and then systematically break it down into smaller,
more manageable bits, which in turn can be tested individually. Children
should be encouraged to use this top-down method of programming. It is
fundamental to LOGO thinking.

Let us take the pattern in figure 9. To reproduce this you need to break it down
into its basic patterns. On closer examination these turn out to be a circle within a
square. The basic pattern is repeated six times. The main procedure should therefore be

```
TO PATTERN

REPEAT 6 (SQ-CIRC RT 60)

END
```

This tells the micro to repeat turns of 60 degrees (since 6 times 60 equals 360)
six times. You still as yet have to define a square with a circle inside.
The next procedure is

```
TO SQ-CIRC

SQ

CIRC

END
```

You draw a square with a circle inside by drawing a square and then a circle.

```
TO SQ

REPEAT 4 (FD 70 RT 90)

END
```

This will draw a square, but how do you fit a circle inside it? The turtle in this
procedure ends up at a corner of the square. In fact you want the turtle to start
and end the square at the centre of a side.

```
TO SQ

REPEAT 4 (FD 35 RT 90 FD 35)

END
```

There are two problems now! How do you draw a circle? How do you draw a
circle that will fit inside the square? A reasonable circle can be drawn by the
procedure

```
TO CIRC

REPEAT 36 (FD 6 RT 10)

END
```

but the circle will not fit the square. The solution is the same as for the square; you start in the centre of the side.

```
TO CIRC

REPEAT 36 (FD 3 RT 10 FD 3 )

END
```

Now try running PATTERN.

The essence of problem-solving in LOGO is to reduce the problem to manageable 'mind-sized' bits. We have worked from an overall view down to the details, by breaking each problem into pieces. Here is a problem that we tackled in the classroom, TO HOUSE. To draw a house Wendy suggested using a square and a triangle for the main structure, with oblongs for windows and a door.

```
TO HOUSE

SQUARE

TRIANGLE

OBLONG1

OBLONG2

END
```

The result of running this program was not a house. Why not? Within the procedure HOUSE, it was necessary to include some commands to place TRIANGLE on top of SQUARE, and to place OBLONG1 and OBLONG2 in their respective positions. I leave you to solve the problem!

With younger children I used the drawings in figures 10-17. Can you draw these?

This is problem-solving. It is personal problem-solving at the child's level. These types of program are pertinent and directly related to what the child knows. They are therefore meaningful and self-motivating. The top-down method of programming in LOGO is an excellent way to teach children a most powerful and useful method of problem-solving.

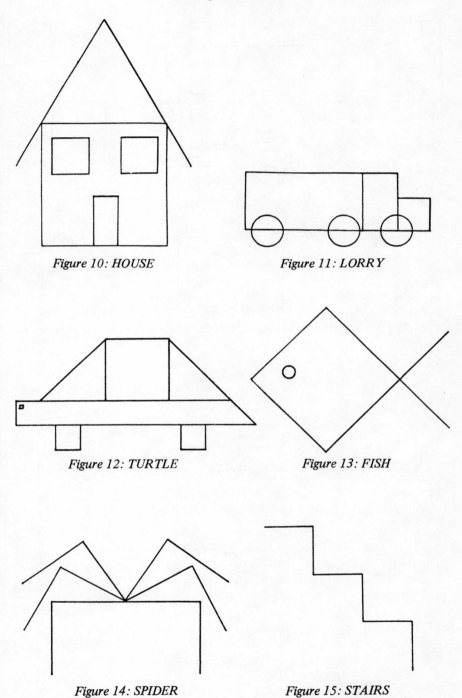

Figure 10: HOUSE

Figure 11: LORRY

Figure 12: TURTLE

Figure 13: FISH

Figure 14: SPIDER

Figure 15: STAIRS

Figure 16: CHICK   *Figure 17: TEDDY BEAR*

8 Recursion

It is possible for a procedure to call itself. This is known as recursion. Recursion opens up endless possibilities for creativity and the exploration of the ideas of spatial geometry. Write any procedure, say

```
TO BLOB

FD 10

LT 45

FD 20

RT 120

FD 20

END
```

This shape is nothing in itself but, if you employ recursion, you get something rather spectacular. After FD 20 insert BLOB and run the program. As the program runs the turtle seems to go on and on. When does it stop? It doesn't; it will not stop unless you switch the machine off or press an appropriate control key. It will continue to repeat itself until the available workspace in the micro has been used up.

Here are some other recursive programs

```
TO DESIGN              TO TWIRLS

SQUARE                 FD 7

LT 135                 REPEAT 8 (FD 4 RT 45)

DESIGN                 TWIRLS

END                    END
```

Children derive a great amount of pleasure from using recursion to find out what a simple procedure or doodle will produce. I used this idea to get them to draw specific shapes such as a circle and regular polygons. Try it yourself. Take a simple procedure and see what it will produce using recursion. Sharif came up with the procedure (figure 18)

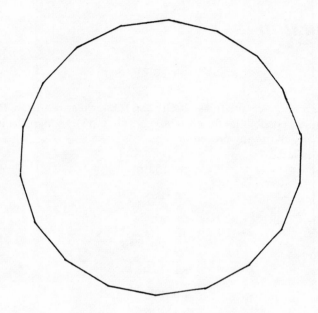

Figure 18: FD 10 RT 20

```
TO SHARIF

FD 10

RT 20

SHARIF

END
```

Recursion is a profound mathematical idea which we have just looked at briefly. If you are already familiar with BASIC, then you should note that recursion is not the same thing as looping, in which the micro goes back to an earlier instruction, but is rather the creation of an entirely new sub-procedure with the same name as the original procedure.

The next example starts with a simple shape and then goes on to use it to make a more interesting shape (figures 19 and 20).

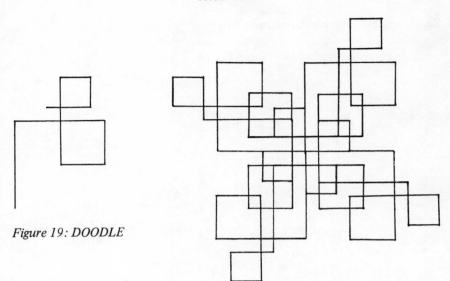

Figure 19: DOODLE

Figure 20: CENGIS

```
TO DOODLE
FD 30
RT 90
FD 30
RT 90
FD 15
RT 90
FD 15
RT 90
FD 30
RT 90
FD 10
RT 90
FD 10
RT 90
FD 15
END
```

```
TO DOT
REPEAT 4 (DOODLE)
END
```

```
TO CENGIS
DOODLE
DOODLE
LEFT 90
CENGIS
END
```

Here is another program that draws a tree

```
TO  HOGWEED  :L

IF  :L<2   THEN  STOP

FD  :L

RT  15

HOGWEED  (3*:L/4)

LT  30

HOGWEED  (3*:L/4)

RT  15

BK  :L

END
```

Why is this 'powerful'?
Why is it good to encounter this 'idea'
in this way?

Having tried out these examples and hopefully a few of your own, you may be still asking yourself some questions. What is the real value of recursion, what is the point of it? Where does it lead to in the classroom? The answer to all these questions is that it leads to familiarity with powerful mathematical ideas at an early and, above all, impressionable age.

Recursion is not just the drawing of complicated patterns, it is a way of thinking — an intellectual exercise. Its outward form is indeed expressed by means of geometry, but the processes underlying this are profound and powerful intellectually. If your child can think procedurally (that is, use recursion and many of the mechanics of LOGO), then he or she is quite a child. He or she *Evidence?* should be able to apply LOGO thinking to other areas of knowledge. We need to teach our children to think, to use their creative powers. One of the ways, I believe, to do this is through LOGO.

9 Variables and Variable Stepping

We have been looking at fixed shapes up to this point. Now I would like to introduce the idea of the variable. Leon drew a square of a given size (FD 50 RT 90). I suggested that he teach the computer to draw squares of various sizes. "This means changing the steps. But how do you tell the computer to change them?". Of course Leon did not know how to do this, but he did understand what was required. My answer was: Play Turtle! You are the turtle. When I give you some commands, I want you to stand still until I give you two input numbers. Are you ready? FORWARD something, LEFT something. Ready? 5,45! Leon moved forward 5 steps and turned 45 degrees to the left. I also tried this approach to variables with younger children, aged five to seven years. It proved to be a popular and successful game (see appendix 1).

Meanwhile back at the computer we decided on the following procedure

TO GROWSQUARE :SIZE

In this procedure a given number of squares would be produced, each one growing in size as the program proceeded. :SIZE is a word for a variable, which we used to determine the size of the squares. The colon (:) is a mathematical symbol for a variable and its adoption by LOGO is therefore very appropriate. Do not leave it out!

On typing GROWSQUARE :SIZE, the computer was told that a procedure was about to be written which would require an input number. If you forget to provide a number, the computer provides a zero value, and nothing appears on the screen.

Next we wrote the statement

```
REPEAT 4 (FD :SIZE RT 90)
```

This simply meant draw four times FORWARD a certain amount (the variable :SIZE) and turn 90 degrees. The final program looked as follows

```
TO GROWSQUARE :SIZE

REPEAT 4 (FD :SIZE RT 90)

END
```

Having established our procedure we typed GROWSQUARE 20. This produced a square 20 steps in size. Leon then continued to type GROWSQUARE followed by a series of input numbers, until he had filled the screen with ever-growing squares. In the procedure GROWSQUARE, Leon used the variable :SIZE with input numbers. This allowed him to draw squares of different sizes. Could other members of the class write one program to draw a series of squares of varying sizes? The answer was yes. They used SQUARE as a sub-procedure of a new procedure called BOXES (figure 21)

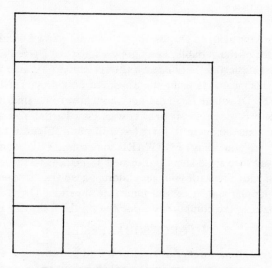

Figure 21: BOXES 10, 20, 30, 40, 50

```
TO BOXES

SQUARE 10

SQUARE 20

SQUARE 30

SQUARE 40

SQUARE 50

END
```

This was not what I wanted, but it worked. I wanted them to use the variable :SIZE. Some of the children were still not ready for variables, they had yet to come to terms with what they had understood so far.

Variations on a Variable

By now you will have realised that ideas in LOGO grow all the time. One idea leads to the next and so on. The following procedure goes a stage further and introduces an additional variable :ANGLE. It uses two inputs, one for :SIZE, the other for :ANGLE.

```
TO FAN :SIZE :ANGLE

FD :SIZE

LT :ANGLE

END
```

If you try running this procedure, the result is rather disappointing. Let us improve on it by using recursion from chapter 8.

```
TO FAN :SIZE :ANGLE

FD :SIZE

LT :ANGLE

FAN :SIZE :ANGLE

END
```

That's much better! The recursion line tells the computer to start a new procedure FAN and so on.

Your Name in Print

You can use any word you like to make a variable. It is important however not to use a LOGO primitive, a word that is part of the computer's basic vocabulary. Some of the children enjoyed using their own names as variables.

```
TO BOYS :WAYNE :GREGORY

FD :WAYNE

LT :GREGORY

BOYS :WAYNE :GREGORY

END


TO GIRLS :RACHEL :LOUISE

REPEAT 2 (FD :RACHEL RT 90 FD :LOUISE RT 90)

END
```

Here are some more ideas using either one or two variables (figure 22).

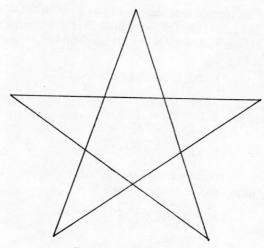

Figure 22: STELLA 50

```
TO STELLA :SIZE
REPEAT 5 (FD :SIZE LT 144)
END


TO SPIN :ANGLE
SQUARE 50
LT :ANGLE
SPIN :ANGLE
END
```

(It is assumed that you have already written a procedure named SQUARE.)

```
TO STARS :ANGLE
FD 30
RT :ANGLE
STARS :ANGLE
END
```

Is there a relationship between the angle input and the final drawing? What does STARS 160 give you?

Teacher's note: You might like to ask the children to draw a table of relationships between the angle input and the number of points of each star.

Using Arithmetical Expressions

The variable :SIZE, or if you prefer :FRED, may be increased or decreased as the program runs. You can use any arithmetical expression to do this. The computer will recognise + and −, but you will have to use * for multiply and / for divide.

```
TO MAGIC-BOX :SIZE

FD :SIZE

RT 90

MAGIC-BOX (:SIZE + 5)

END
```

```
TO ZX :SIDE :ANGLE

FD :SIDE

LT :ANGLE

ZX (:SIDE*2) :ANGLE

END
```

```
TO ARGONAUTS :JASON1 :JASON2

FD :JASON1

LT :JASON2

ARGONAUTS (:JASON1 - 10) :JASON2

END
```

If you enter ARGONAUTS 100, 45 the pattern on the screen is drawn in reverse. In all these programs the recursion seems to go on for ever. What happens if you want to stop at a certain point in the program? The way to do this is to use the conditional statement IF followed by STOP.

```
IF :SIZE > 100 STOP
IF :SIZE < 10 STOP


TO MAZE :SIZE
IF :SIZE > 100 STOP
FD :SIZE
LT 90
MAZE (:SIZE + 3)
END
```

Every time the program reaches the recursion line

$$MAZE (:SIZE + 3)$$

the size is increased by 3. When it reaches 100, the job is done and the program stops.

Local and Global Variables

Variables such as :SIZE, :ANGLE or :SEAN that are written on the same line as the TO statement are local to the procedure; that is, they belong or are specific to the procedure and to no other. For example, in

TO SUNFLOWER :SIZE :ANGLE

the variables :SIZE and :ANGLE in the procedure SUNFLOWER belong exclusively to SUNFLOWER.

Take another procedure

TO DAISY :SIZE :ANGLE

In both DAISY and SUNFLOWER we find the variables :SIZE and :ANGLE. They are not however identical. The :SIZE and :ANGLE of DAISY are not the same as the :SIZE and :ANGLE of SUNFLOWER. There are :SIZE and :ANGLE that belong to SUNFLOWER, and :SIZE and :ANGLE that belong to DAISY. Never the twain shall meet. Each of these variables is kept in its own memory location, so there is no confusion between the variables of DAISY and the variables of SUNFLOWER.

On the other hand, global variables created in a procedure belong automatically to a common memory location. They are created by using the MAKE statement

```
MAKE "SIZE 50
```

and placing them within the procedure instead of in the TO statement

```
TO SEASCAPE            TO LANDSCAPE

MAKE "SIZE 50          FD :SIZE

FD :SIZE
```

The variable :SIZE with the value 50 is now common to both procedures. In LANDSCAPE, the turtle will move forward 50 steps. There is therefore only one storage location assigned to each particular global variable.

All references to these global variables in fact refer to the same storage location even if the references are in different procedures. This provides a means of sharing information among procedures or among turtles (if the LOGO has multiple turtles as in TANDY LOGO). Since :SIZE is not written on the TO statement, it therefore belongs to the general memory of the computer. Until deleted or changed, :SIZE will always be 50.

LOGO uses (") and (:) to signify variables. "SIZE tells the computer the name of the variable, while :SIZE is its value, in this case 50

```
"SIZE                  the name of the variable

:SIZE                  the value of the variable
```

Here are some more examples

```
MAKE "ANGLE 72         MAKE "LENGTH 100

LT :ANGLE              BK :LENGTH
```

The turtle will now turn left 72 degrees and move backwards 100 steps.

Every time that you use MAKE and (") you are making a new variable, and whenever you type (:) followed by the new variable you are asking the computer to output its value. The best way to distinguish between local and global variables, between (") and (:), is to experiment and use them.

LOGO is a practical approach to abstract ideas. It allows children to concretise formal or abstract concepts. Jasmin may not be able to write an essay on variable stepping, but she knows how to make use of a very powerful idea.

10 Polyworlds

Regular Polygons

Some of the programs in this chapter were written by individual children, while others were the result of group sessions with me in the role of teacher and referee. We worked in groups of four. Two procedures that are very popular in the classroom are POLY and POLYSPI. These are procedures that draw amazing polygons and spirals, by means of variables. The rule for POLY is forward a fixed amount, turn right or left a fixed amount and repeat this sequence over and over again.

```
TO POLY :SIZE :ANGLE

FD :SIZE

LT :ANGLE

POLY :SIZE :ANGLE

END
```

The children then began experimenting with different inputs (figures 23 and 24).

POLY 10 90	POLY 10 60	POLY 20 135
POLY 50 72	POLY 60 144	POLY 30 108
POLY 50 160	POLY 60 80	POLY 80 144

You will have noticed that these figures drawn by POLY always close. However the number of sides that must be drawn before the figure closes depends on the ANGLE input. Further ideas for exploration are discussed in Part 4 (LOGO Workshop). Try some variations on POLY using a sub-procedure, such as TRIANGLE or OBLONG, to replace FD and ANGLE.

From POLY we went on to POLYSPI. This is a variant of POLY. It uses recursion to increase the turtle's forward step each time the procedure calls itself. The result is a polygonal spiral (figures 25-27).

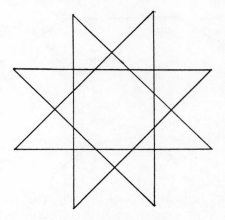

Figure 23: POLY 20 135

Figure 24: POLY 30 108

```
TO POLYSPI :SIZE :ANGLE
FD :SIZE
LT :ANGLE
POLYSPI (:SIZE+3) :ANGLE
END
```

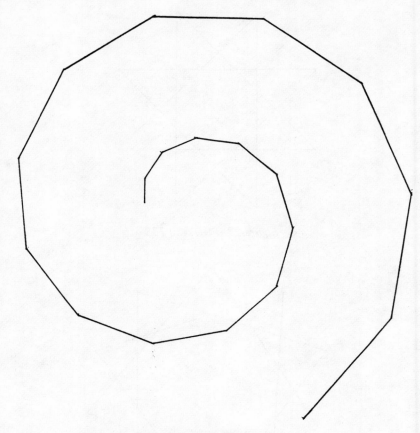

Figure 25: POLYSPI 10 32 5

Try POLYSPI with these inputs

             1 120   0 90   1 45

and again

```
TO POLYSPI :SIZE :ANGLE
IF :SIZE> 100 STOP
FD :SIZE
RT :ANGLE
POLYSPI (:SIZE+5) :ANGLE
END
```

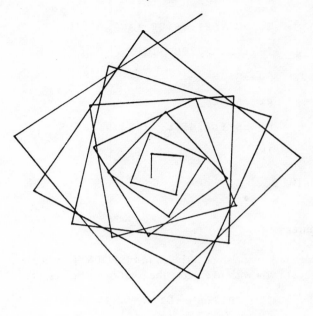

Figure 26: POLYSPI 10 95 3

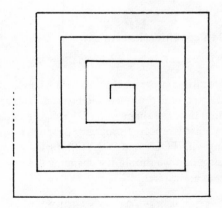

Figure 27: POLYSPI 5 90 5

The forward step is now increased by 5 each time until 100 is reached.

Conversely you can decrease the steps of the spiral. Increments can also be expressed in terms of a variable.

```
TO POLYSPI :SIZE :ANGLE :INC

IF :SIZE> 200 STOP

FD :SIZE

RT :ANGLE

POLYSPI (:SIZE+ :INC) :ANGLE :INC

END
```

Try this with 10 32 5.

Rotating Figures

Previous procedures may also be included in the POLYSPI procedure. This is very useful should you wish to explore the rotation of figures.

```
TO TRIPLES :SIZE :ANGLE

TRIANGLE :SIZE

RT :ANGLE

TRIPLES (:SIZE + 1) :ANGLE

END
```

You can of course add a conditional statement

```
IF :SIZE  >  100 STOP
```

TRIPLES is a simple recursive program that draws a triangle of a given size, rotates it, increases the size, and continues the process. You might like to discuss with the children how the shape of a POLY figure depends on the angle input and why so many repeated programs produce symmetrical designs.

After experimenting with POLY and POLYSPI during many sessions on the computer, Kate suggested we should try changing the angle. This produced a figure that is known as an inspiral.

```
TO INSPI :SIZE :ANGLE

FD :SIZE

RT :ANGLE

INSPI :SIZE (:ANGLE + 10)

END
```

Kate tried the following

```
INSPI 20 10 and 20 33
```

She went on to use INC and DEC as variables.

```
TO INSPI :SIZE :ANGLE :INC

FD :SIZE

LT :ANGLE

INSPI :SIZE (:ANGLE + :INC) :INC

END
```

```
TO INSPI :SIZE :ANGLE :DEC

FD :SIZE

RT :ANGLE

INSPI :SIZE (:ANGLE - :DEC) :DEC

END
```

Another useful procedure we wrote as a group was TTT, which drew regular polygons on request.

```
TO TTT :SIDE :SIZE

REPEAT :SIDE (FD :SIZE RT 360/:SIDE)

END
```

More Spirals

The previous procedure for drawing regular polygons used angle inputs that were multiples of 360. It is also interesting to use angle inputs that are slightly below or above these inputs. Instead of 45 to produce an octagon, use 44 or 46. Instead of 72 to produce a pentagon, try 71 or 73.

Again, instead of POLYSPI, you can create spirals by using variables with REPEAT. To create the variable you have to use MAKE.

```
MAKE "D 1

REPEAT 250 (FD :D RT 71 MAKE "D :D+3)
```

or

```
MAKE "A 0

REPEAT 500 (FD 5 RT :A MAKE "A :A+10)
```

To complete this chapter, here is a curious program that draws a spiral that is shared between two procedures. Where does it begin? I was going to call it 'You-scratch-my-back' but decided that A and B would be simpler.

```
TO A

MAKE "SIZE :SIZE + 1

FD :SIZE LT 45

B


TO B

FD :SIZE

RT 90

IF :SIZE > 40 THEN STOP

A
```

:SIZE has the default value of 0. Try experimenting with similar programs yourself. Could you write a program that used three interrelated procedures?

11 Curves

A Different Geometry

If you draw a circle by means of coordinate geometry, you are obliged to refer to a global coordinate system or, if you prefer the Euclidean method, you have to refer to some fixed point. Both methods are nevertheless dependent on a fixed global reference. The turtle method of drawing a circle is both intrinsic and local. This means that when you draw a circle on the screen with the turtle, you do not have to refer to a fixed point as in Euclidean geometry, nor on the other hand are you obliged to refer to a global coordinate system, as you would be if you were using coordinate geometry. On the contrary, as the turtle draws on the screen, it moves only in relation to itself. The turtle is concerned only with its own current position and heading. As it draws, it can ignore the rest of the plane that surrounds its current position and draw what it sets out to represent, piece by piece. Without a special point of reference, the turtle is also free to escape from plane geometry to that intriguing world of curvature and topology.

Again Turtle Geometry describes geometric objects in terms of procedures rather than equations. This procedural approach allows the use of iteration (repetition) for example, which is difficult to use with traditional algebra. Moreover it allows you to explore many important ideas in mathematics such as vectors, curved space and general relativity.

Normally if you want to draw a circle you either draw around a coin or use a compass. I asked the children to draw a circle on the screen. This they found very difficult to do, until they Played Turtle. It was only after several attempts that Sharif managed to do it. He discovered that to make a circle you have to walk repeatedly forward a little and turn a little. A circle was made up of little steps such as FD 1 RT 1.

In Play Turtle, the children were familiar with the Total Turtle Trip or TTT for short. Moving from the starting point (HOME) by a succession of FDs and RTs or LTs always brings the turtle back to its original position. The amount of turn was always 360 degrees or multiples of this value. On the screen Sharif moved the turtle repeatedly FD 10 and RT 20. The children soon discovered that any combination of small numbers would produce a circle. Of course what they actually produced were regular 360gons. But how to write a procedure? This is where TTT came to the rescue.

```
TO CIRCLE

REPEAT 360 (FD 1 RT 1)
```

or

```
REPEAT 36 (FD 10 RT 10)
```

If a circle is 360, half a circle must be 180, and half again must be 90. This led to the discovery of arcs.

```
TO ARCR

REPEAT 180 (FD 10 RT 20)

END
```

```
TO ARCL

REPEAT 90 (FD 10 LT 20)

END
```

What we had learnt in previous sessions could now be applied to a procedure called CIRCLE (figure 28).

```
TO CIRCLE1 :SIZE

REPEAT 36 (FD :SIZE RT 10)

END
```

Figure 28: CIRCLE

The children now had new building blocks with which to explore curves. Unfortunately they could not do much with them, since to study curves successfully you inevitably have to introduce pi. Some LOGOs cannot handle decimals and therefore you are limited in this area.

Using Pi

For older children the next procedure uses the formula $2\pi/360 = 0.0174$. The circumference of the circle is 360 units and therefore the radius (R) must ꞵe 360 divided by 2π. To draw a fairly accurate circle, the turtle must move forward by $2\pi R/360$ for each step, and turn by 1 degree.

```
TO CIRCLE :RADIUS

REPEAT 360 (FD :RADIUS * 0.0174 RT 1)

END
```

12 LOGO Arithmetic

LOGO is not only Turtle Geometry. It also has the ability to manipulate number. The micro can be used as a calculator.

PRINT 10 + 6

PRINT 28 - 7

PRINT 30 * 5   (* is used in place of x, to distinguish
                    it from the letter ´X´)

PRINT 360/6   (/ is the computer symbol for division)

Parentheses can also be employed

PRINT 3(10 + 17) * 20

A variety of calculations can be carried out using LOGO, either individually or in a procedure. In procedures such as POLYSPI or INSPI, numbers have been used as inputs. You can also make a procedure OUTPUT a value, or in other words, provide you with a result.

This is a simple program to find the average of certain numbers.

TO AVERAGE :A :B

OUTPUT (:A + :B)/2

END

You can either type **AVERAGE 80 40** and receive the answer 60, or you can use the PRINT statement

PRINT (AVERAGE 80 40)

answer 60

PRINT (AVERAGE 6 8)

answer 7

PRINT (AVERAGE 7 9) + (AVERAGE 10 14)

?

PRINT (AVERAGE(AVERAGE 4 5)6)

?

58

I used the next two programs as a way of introducing arithmetical procedures.

```
TO ADD :X :Y

OUTPUT (:X + :Y)

END


TO SUBTRACT :A :B

OUTPUT (:A - :B)

END
```

You may want a program that will help children learn their tables by counting on. The multiples of a number are printed in a column down the screen.

```
1. TO COUNT-ON :NUM

2. PRINT :ANS

3. MAKE "ANS :ANS + :NUM

4. HT

5. PU BK 8 PD

6. IF :ANS > 144 THEN STOP

7. COUNT-ON :NUM

8. END
```

Although lines are not numbered in LOGO I have included them here to explain the program.

1. Name of procedure.
2. This line prints the answer.
3. :ANS is the value of the variable "ANS, which is added to your input number :NUM.
4. Hides the turtle so that you can see the figures more clearly on the screen.
5. Moves the turtle in order to print the figures down the screen.
6. The conditional statement that controls how far you wish to count. This can of course be changed to any number you wish.
7. Recursion — returns to the beginning of the program.

Since :ANS is not given a specific value, it takes 0 as a default value. This default facility is very useful for building up increments from within a program.

The next program combines Turtle Geometry and number. As the turtle draws a shape, the number of times it draws a particular shape is recorded on the screen. I found this program useful for keeping count of lengthy investigations into open and closed figures.

The control program is called MEANDER. This does the counting and stops the drawing by referring to the turtle's heading at zero (that is, facing up the screen).

```
TO MEANDER

SCRIBBLE

MAKE :NUM :NUM + 1

PRINT :NUM

IF HEADING = 0 THEN STOP

MEANDER
```

The drawing is carried out by SCRIBBLE

```
TO SCRIBBLE

FD 15 LT 144 FD 30 LT 144

FD 45 LT 144 FD 60 RT 144

FD 75 LT 144 FD 10 LT 144

HT

END
```

There are endless possibilities here and I am sure many teachers will invent other programs that make use of the basic skills of number. The children themselves will certainly find number work more rewarding if they are free to write their own programs.

PART 3: LOGO LEARNING — LIST PROCESSING

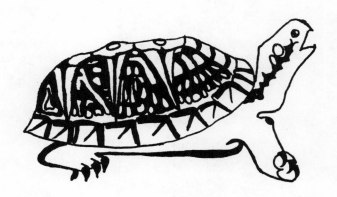

13 A Simple Database

In addition to Turtle Geometry and manipulating number, LOGO can also be used for data processing. Information fed into the computer can be processed in a variety of ways. It can be stored, changed or printed out. The data or information handled by LOGO is of three different kinds: numbers, words and lists. Handling lists is called list processing. It is a very sophisticated process which is used extensively in Artificial Intelligence and robotics, but through LOGO can be used for early language development with infants. LOGO is in fact derived from LISP (List Processing), which was developed in the USA. Although LISP is one of the oldest programming languages, it is still very forward-looking and extremely versatile. It has been used for a variety of subjects, from designing integrated circuits to writing computer games. It is ideal for writing interactive programs, a feature that it has passed on to LOGO.

I used an aspect of LISP for language development with five and six-year-olds. I wanted the children to build up a simple database by writing words at the keyboard and then retrieving them for their sentence-making. I always teach in an open situation, in which the children work in groups on different activities at the same time. This allows me to work with an individual group containing about four to five children. The other children have their own assignments, which leaves me free to concentrate on any one particular group.

I began with a theme called ZOO. Using LISP, I typed

```
(SETQ ZOO '(
```

I then asked Matthew (5 years old) to type in the name of an animal. He chose ELEPHANT. I had to spell it for him, as I did for the names chosen by the others. I then asked Gregory to name another animal and so on. The final program was

```
(SETQ ZOO   (ELEPHANT BEAR MONKEY GIRAFFE LION))
```

SETQ is used to give the variable ZOO a value which will be a list of animals. I again asked Matthew to type the word ZOO. The computer printed out the list of animals

```
(ELEPHANT BEAR MONKEY GIRAFFE LION)
```

We then saved this and other similar lists, or sets as I called them, on tape.

Later when the children wanted to write something about the ZOO or FARM they could refer to their database for the names of animals and their spellings.

The MAKE Game

Using LOGO I introduced the children to the MAKE statement. This is roughly equivalent to SETQ. It does the same job and is more intelligible for infant programmers.

```
MAKE "ZOO (Elephant Bear Monkey Giraffe Lion)
```

I called this the MAKE Game, relating it to sets. Make a set of shapes

```
MAKE "SHAPES (Triangle Square Oblong Circle)
```

Make a set of cars

```
MAKE "CARS (Mini Datsun Polski-Fiat Ford)
```

For topic work with older children we used the MAKE Game to build lists of useful words

```
MAKE "RAIN-WORDS (splash puddle drops sparkle grey-skies)
MAKE WINTER-WORDS (ice freezing snowflake white
                   frosty cold)
```

To retrieve these lists of words, all you have to do is type

```
PRINT :RAIN-WORDS

PRINT :WINTER-WORDS

PRINT :CARS

PRINT :ZOO

PRINT :SHAPES
```

From these examples it can be seen that MAKE needs two inputs. The first is the name of the variable (ZOO) which must be preceded by ("), while the second input is the value of the variable (the list of animals). The variable can also be a word or a number. Whenever you create a new word in the MAKE statement, you must use (") to precede it. Thus "ABC123 or "+/a6 are both regarded as words in LOGO.

```
MAKE "XY211 (50 BANANAS)

PRINT :XY211


> 50 BANANAS
```

Variables

It is important to be able to distinguish between "ZOO and :ZOO. The symbol (") is the name of the set or package. The (:) is its value or contents. Thus

"ZOO is the *name* of the set of animals

:ZOO is its value, or in other words the list of animals contained in
the set

When you type PRINT :ZOO or PRINT :CARS, the computer prints out the contents of ZOO or CARS.

I do not assume that infants will understand how the MAKE Game works. In fact some eyebrows were raised at the very idea of using list processing in the first school. However it works, and the children are at least exposed to the ideas of list processing, even if they do not understand the underlying principles. If you think that your children will be confused by the computer keyboard, then just let them have a go and see for yourself. I am convinced that children both enjoy pressing buttons, however long it might take to produce a word, and that they are sticklers for precision – they will not fail to notice if you leave out (") or (:), or press the return key too soon. And there is always the wise guy or doll who is already on to the next stage of your scheme even before you are! So give it a try.

Most primary school classrooms have or should have a word bank. This is usually a wall display in which useful and specific project/topic words are stored for reference by the children. The word bank is in computer terms a data bank. Words for such topics as weather or the home (as illustrated in the MAKE Game) can be displayed and stored in the classroom. The computer can be used in a similar way. It does not however replace the word bank. On the contrary it reinforces it, by providing a useful tool for language development. Children should be encouraged to use the computer to develop their language, through sorting and classification. They can work on a class project or individually. Even very young infants, as in the MAKE Game, can use the computer in this way. They can use it to learn new words and above all to handle them through the writing of simple procedures for the data bank. This activity in itself promotes computer literacy.

A further development of the MAKE Game is the following procedure

```
TO BALLET STARS          TO ROMAN DRESS

PRINT (ANNA PAVLOVA)     PRINT (TOGA)

      (BERYL GREY)             (TUNICA)

      (NIJINSKY)              (STOLA)

      (   )                    (   )

END                      END
```

Children are given words which they have to classify. This can be done as a group or a class activity, or as part of individual learning. The procedures are similar to those used for Turtle Geometry. Information is stored in the parentheses (). On typing BALLET STARS or ROMAN DRESS, the computer prints out the stored data.

TO FLOWERS	TO COLOURS	TO LITTORINA
PRINT (DAFFODIL)	PRINT (RED)	PRINT (NERITOIDES)
(ROSE)	(GREEN)	(RUDIS)
(POPPY)	(BLUE)	(LITTORALIS)
( )	( )	( )
END	END	END

For example, infants can use these procedures to record new words or ideas for story-writing. Again I find it useful to approach this type of classification through sets. I ask the children to write a procedure to make a set of farm animals, vehicles or buildings. These programs can be adapted for any level, from infants (the procedure COLOURS) to secondary pupils (LITTORINA) depending on the subject or area of the curriculum. Using the computer for such procedures might seem to you to be rather a waste of an expensive piece of machinery. Such procedures are indeed very limited. The information that they produce cannot be manipulated or processed. To process these collections of data, you need a different tool. This tool is list processing.

What is a List?

Briefly a list is a sequence of information or data, usually words that have been combined into groups or sets. We have already used lists in the MAKE Game

(ELEPHANT BEAR MONKEY GIRAFFE LION)·

This is a list containing five items or members. The following

((JOHN SMITH) SALLY NIKOLAI)

is a list containing three items. In this example the items in a list can themselves be lists. I suppose it is a little like the poem about fleas having fleas and so on *ad infinitum.*

How many items are in this list?

((TED BROWN) RACHEL GREGORY (SARAH FRANCES))

The answer is four. Here are some more examples

(1 2 3 4)	Four members
(1 2 (3 4))	Three members
(A 2 B 5)	Four members
(a (2 b 5))	Two members
( )	No members

The last example is called an empty list or, in mathematics, the empty set. (The theory of list processing tends to be a brain teaser! If you find it difficult to follow, stop and tackle each new operator or statement individually. Try it out on the keyboard before proceeding to the next operator or statement. I would advise you not to cover too much of the theory at once, but to test each area by making up your own examples.)

14 Interactive Programs

With older children, procedures can be used to create interactive programs. I find in my own teaching that the best way is to get a group of children to write a quiz program or similar interactive programs for the other members of the class.

```
TO GOSSIP

PRINT (TELL ME SOMETHING YOU DID TODAY)

PRINT SE (I'M GLAD YOU ) REQUEST

END
```

The operator SENTENCE or SE (see chapter 15) outputs the list (I'M GLAD YOU) together with the output of the word REQUEST.

REQUEST is another LOGO command that waits for you to type a line, in this case a response to the computer's request, and then outputs that line as a list. It makes it easy for you to write interactive programs using lists.

```
TO QUIZ1

MAKE "NUM1 RANDOM 100

MAKE "NUM2 RANDOM 100

MAKE "ANSWER :NUM1 + :NUM2

PRINT (SENTENCE (HOW MUCH IS) :NUM1

(+) :NUM2)

MAKE "REPLY REQUEST

TEST :REPLY = :ANSWER

IFTRUE PRINT (GOOD)

IFFALSE PRINT SENTENCE (THE ANSWER IS ) :ANSWER

QUIZ

END
```

This program chooses two numbers at random and prints them on the screen as an addition sentence. The computer waits for you to type in the answer. If you are correct, GOOD appears on the screen. If you type in a wrong answer, the computer tells you the correct answer. The word TEST checks to see if your reply tallies with the correct answer. IFTRUE and IFFALSE evaluate the answer and print the list contained in parentheses.

```
TO ROMANS

PRINT (WHO WAS GOVERNOR OF BRITAIN DURING THE REIGN OF
    BOADICEA?)

IF REQUEST=(PAULINUS) THEN PRINT (YES THAT´S CORRECT!)
    STOP

PRINT (NO, TRY AGAIN)

ROMANS

END
```

This program like the number quiz uses a conditional statement

```
        IF REQUEST = ...THEN PRINT
```

Note also the use of recursion, ROMANS, which enables the program to continue until the correct answer is given.

Quiz programs are for the children to write themselves. They are not for adults to use as computer assisted learning (CAL). Thus the program ROMANS is not a sophisticated program. For a child to write a simple quiz program means that he or she has to do a lot of thinking. It involves both skilful programming and imagination. In particular children have to learn to manipulate lists (see chapter 15), which in itself is a skill that demands precision and clear thinking. It is therefore quite an achievement for someone like Wendy or Leon to produce a few lines of an interactive program in LOGO. To design a complete quiz program is, in my opinion, the crowning achievement of list processing for children. With a few basic tools and plenty of imagination, the prospects are virtually unlimited.

This approach to computing, and indeed the whole of learning, is central to the philosophy of LOGO. Without this exploratory and procedural approach to problem-solving, LOGO is not LOGO: it is an impoverished exercise in formal logic. Therefore to help resist any temptation to use these programs to cram in as much information as you can, I have avoided producing 'finished' programs. By all means develop your own, but remember, LOGO is for children to use creatively and imaginatively as young programmers, not as passive recipients of computerised drill and practice.

15 Manipulating Lists

LOGO employs certain command words or operators that can manipulate lists. Here are some of them

FIRST	WORD
BUTFIRST	SENTENCE
LAST	
BUTLAST	

Sometimes you will find it necessary to retrieve or output certain members of lists. This is a useful exercise for language development and I have used it with top infants. The children are asked to think of a word, say for a set of shapes, which they then type into the computer. Having built the set, such as

```
MAKE "SHAPES (TRIANGLE CIRCLE OBLONG SQUARE)
```

each child is asked to retrieve or output his word. Using the operators listed above we can extract the individual members of the list as follows

```
PRINT FIRST :SHAPES
```

This extracts TRIANGLE from the list of shapes.

But how do we extract the others? This is done by using the other operators in various combinations. To extract CIRCLE, you type

```
PRINT FIRST BUTFIRST :SHAPES
```

This gives you CIRCLE.

```
PRINT LAST BUTLAST :SHAPES
```

This gives you OBLONG.

```
PRINT LAST :SHAPES
```

This gives the last item of your list: SQUARE.

The children with whom I used these operators did not understand the logic. As far as they were concerned, typing LAST BUTLAST or FIRST BUTFIRST was just a means to an end. They were more interested in manipulating their own word. But at the same time they were using advanced techniques in list processing, which later they would use and understand intuitively. It is this kind of intuitive learning that is vital to LOGO learning and which I believe is instrumental in creating a rich learning environment for the future.

List manipulation can also be used with or without procedures. You do not have to use the MAKE statement every time but can simply use the operators as follows

```
PRINT FIRST (DAISY ROSE TULIP)

>DAISY
```

The word DAISY is extracted from the list of flowers.

```
PRINT FIRST ((JOHN SMITH) KEVIN JANE)

>JOHN SMITH
```

In this example the output is JOHN SMITH, which is not a word but a list containing two words — JOHN and SMITH. They are placed in parentheses to indicate that (JOHN SMITH) is a list.

```
PRINT LAST (APPLE PEAR ORANGE GRAPE)

>GRAPE
```

This outputs the word GRAPE.

```
PRINT BUTFIRST (ANT BEETLE BEE)


>BEETLE BEE
```

This time all but the first word are extracted from the list — that is, the remainder of the list of insects.

```
PRINT BUTLAST (CEDAR OAK BEECH LARCH)

>CEDAR OAK BEECH
```

Here all but the last word are extracted from the list of trees. If we return to RAIN-WORDS in chapter 13, we can ask each child to retrieve his word from the list. To make the list

```
Kevin typed  SPLASH      (SPLASH

Maureen typed PUDDLE     (SPLASH PUDDLE

Amarjit typed DROPS      (SPLASH PUDDLE DROPS)
```

We now ask the children to retrieve their words.

```
        Kevin types FIRST :RAIN-WORDS
```

This outputs Kevin's word SPLASH.

```
        Maureen types LAST BUTLAST :RAIN-WORDS
```

This outputs Maureen's word PUDDLE.

```
        Amarjit types LAST :RAIN-WORDS
```

and retrieves his word DROPS.

The Use of SENTENCE (SE)

In the interactive programs in chapter 14 the operator SENTENCE or SE was
used to output the lists in those programs. SENTENCE takes a number of lists
and puts them together to make a single list.

```
        SENTENCE (CHARLIE BROWN)  (SNOOPY LINUS)

        >CHARLIE BROWN SNOOPY LINUS.
```

The two lists are combined by SENTENCE to form one large list. In the
GOSSIP program we had the following line

```
        PRINT SENTENCE (I´M GLAD YOU) REQUEST
```

Here SENTENCE combines the two lists (I'M GLAD YOU) and the reply,
which is indicated by the word REQUEST. The final output is one large list,
such as

```
        I´M GLAD YOU DID ʼNOTHING
```


Words and Lists

So far we have been using operators with lists. We can however use these same
operators to manipulate words.

```
        PRINT SENTENCE "AN (APPLE A DAY)

        >AN APPLE A DAY
```

SENTENCE combines the word "AN and the list (APPLE A DAY)

```
        PRINT SE (THE FIRST DAY OF) "SPRING

        >THE FIRST DAY OF SPRING

        PRINT SE "WELL "DONE

        >WELL DONE
```

SENTENCE normally has two inputs, but it can have more if the command and the inputs are placed within parentheses.

```
PRINT (SE (THE FIRST DAY) "OF "SPRING)

>THE FIRST DAY OF SPRING
```

The Use of WORD

The operator WORD takes two words as inputs and produces or outputs the combination as one large word

```
PRINT WORD "WO "RD        = WORD

PRINT WORD "CROSS "WORD   = CROSSWORD

PRINT WORD "TIME "TABLE   = TIMETABLE
```

If you place the operator and the inputs in parentheses, then the operator WORD can have more than two inputs.

```
PRINT (WORD "MICRO "CHIL "DREN )
```

Do not forget to leave a space after DREN or the last) will be included in the final word MICROCHILDREN.

Using Operators with Words

To manipulate the letters or symbols of a word, you can use the same operators that you used for lists.

```
PRINT FIRST "ABCD

>A
```

This outputs the first letter of the word.

```
PRINT BUTFIRST "ABCD

>BCD
```

All but the first letter are extracted from the word.

```
PRINT LAST "ABCD

>D
```

The last letter of the word is extracted.

```
PRINT BUTLAST "ABCD
>ABC
```

All but the last are extracted from the word "ABCD.

You can also combine the operators to manipulate words.

```
PRINT LAST BUTLAST "ABCD
>C
PRINT BUTFIRST "A
>( )
```

This outputs an empty word — that is, nothing at all.

Try some examples yourself.

```
PRINT FIRST "MATTHEW
PRINT BUTFIRST "MATTHEW
PRINT LAST "MATTHEW
PRINT BUTLAST "MATTHEW
```

Now make some more of your own.

If you have managed to follow these examples so far, try this

```
PRINT FIRST BUTFIRST (THE LAST DAY OF SUMMER)
```

This example outputs the second word of the list. In LOGO jargon, OUTPUT means to send a message with information — that is, a result. The information must be a number, word or list. It is the opposite of INPUT, whereby you put data into the program as in the turtle programs POLY :SIZE.

Using OUTPUT means that you want the computer to produce a result. To return to LOGO arithmetic, let us look at the following program to produce the square of a number

```
TO SQ:A
OUTPUT :A * :A
END
```

If you type SQ 3, the computer will output

```
>9
```

or if you type SQ 4, the computer will output

```
>16
```

In this chapter we have built up a basic tool-kit for manipulating lists. Putting some of the tools together you are now able to write a procedure that will manipulate lists.

```
TO DOUBLE :L

OUTPUT SENTENCE :L : L

END
```

Now type PRINT DOUBLE (JOHN SMITH)

= JOHN SMITH JOHN SMITH

Now type once more PRINT DOUBLE DOUBLE (JOHN SMITH)

= JOHN SMITH JOHN SMITH JOHN SMITH JOHN SMITH

Further Use of Variables

In chapter 9 variables were used to control or change the size or shape of turtle procedures. As we saw in the MAKE Game, words and lists can also be used as variables. They can be assigned names and stored in the computer's memory. This can be done by using them as inputs to a procedure.

```
TO NEWS :ITEM

PRINT (TODAY'S NEWS IS )

PRINT :ITEM

END
```

The variable or input :ITEM can be a word, a list or a number, depending in this case on the context or meaning.

Type NEWS (CLASS 6 WILL PLAY FOOTBALL THIS AFTERNOON)

Type NEWS (SCHOOL WILL FINISH AT 2.30)

The next program uses: (1) the operator BUTFIRST, (2) the variable "A, and (3) its value :A, which is the list of flowers (POPPY DAISY BUTTERCUP ROSE).

```
TO FLOWERS :A

MAKE "A (POPPY DAISY BUTTERCUP ROSE)

PRINT BUTFIRST :A

END

>DAISY BUTTERCUP ROSE
```

The next procedure uses the BUTFIRST operator and a conditional statement.

```
TO TRIANGLE :SCATTER

IF :SCATTER = " THEN STOP

PRINT :SCATTER

TRIANGLE BUTFIRST :SCATTER

END
```

The space after " is an empty word; if there are no more letters left, the program stops. This is also another example of recursion

potatoes	constantinople
otatoes	onstantinople
tatoes	nstantinople
atoes	stantinople
toes	tantinople
oes	antinople
es	ntinople
s	tinople
	inople
	nople
	ople
	ple
	le
	e

The program continues to run until the BUTFIRST operator reads the (") empty word.

PART 4: LOGO WORKSHOP

16 Turtle Projects

In this part of the book I would like you to join me in an exploration of Turtle Geometry and some elementary features of list processing.

Using RANDOM

To begin, let us look at a LOGO word called RANDOM. As always, it is a good idea for you to try using RANDOM in as many ways as you can. In fact what I offer you here only scratches the surface of much greater ideas in computational geometry and Artificial Intelligence.

In this workshop you will find an 'intelligent' program that enables you to hold a conversation with your micro, and a simulation of simple animal behaviour. But before you start teaching your machine to talk or embark on a study of paramecia, let us explore with the turtle.

RANDOM takes an input integer or whole number, say 30, which in turn tells the computer to output any number from 0 to 29. You can use RANDOM followed by any integer, depending on the capability of your computer. RANDOM can be used in a variety of situations, as the following programs will demonstrate.

Regular figures
RANDOM is used for the steps of the turtle; the angle remains fixed.

```
TO B

REPEAT 4 (FD RANDOM 100 LT 72)

END


TO STEPS

FD RANDOM 50 RT 90

FD RANDOM 50 LT 90

STEPS
```

```
TO TRI

REPEAT 20 (MAKE "S1 RANDOM 100

REPEAT 3 (FD :S1 RT 120)

FD RANDOM 50 RT 45

FD RANDOM 50 LT 45

END
```

```
TO OCTO

MAKE "TURN RANDOM 20

REPEAT 10 (FD :TURN LT 45)

END
```

```
TO BUBBLES

REPEAT RANDOM 50 (OCTO)

PU FD 20 PD

BUBBLES

END
```

Change the number after RANDOM and see what happens.
   The next program might be used by DIY robots to decorate your bathroom

```
TO SCAFFOLDING

FD RANDOM 50 RT 90

FD RANDOM 50 RT 90

SCAFFOLDING

END
```

Irregular figures
This time RANDOM is used for the angle with a fixed step. We also add
recursion to the procedure.

```
TO MAP

REPEAT 200 (FD 5 LT RANDOM 360)

MAP

END
```

WALKABOUT

From early times, mathematicians have studied such things as number pattern and geometrical relationships. Exploration is indeed fundamental to mathematical thinking and, thanks to LOGO, young children can carry out mathematical investigations in the true spirit of the ancient Greeks or their modern counterparts! The following exercises are a mathematical investigation into patterns generated by a WALKABOUT on the screen.

Continue the pattern

```
FD 10 RT 90 FD 20 RT 90 FD 30 RT 90
```

Repeat this sequence, always returning to FD 10, until you produce a closed figure on the screen. The first rule is forward one step, two steps, three steps. The second rule is one step, two steps, three steps, four steps. Now change the rule by increasing the steps to five, each time remembering to put in the angle of 90 degrees (or the angle of your choice) between the steps.

Continue the pattern

```
FD 10 LT 120 FD 20 LT 120 FD 30 LT 120...
```

The rule is one step, two steps, three steps repeated with the angle in between.

```
FD 10 LT 120 FD 20 LT 120 FD 30 LT 120 FD 40 LT 120 ....
```

Increase the rule up to 12 steps or FD 120! How many open figures do you produce? How many closed figures? Is there a pattern to be found? Try alternating LT and RT for instance, or use RT 120 after FD 30 and use RT 120 after FD 60 in longer sequences. The value of the exercise is to teach children to look for patterns and relationships, and at the same time to develop their powers of investigation and inductive reasoning. Can you predict what the next shape will be?

Some children have an eye for pattern, while others need to develop this skill. This type of LOGO investigation teaches such a skill in a systematic and practical way. The patterns produced are known as spirolaterals (figures 29–31).

Biology Lesson

The world about us provides a rich environment for the study of animal behaviour. If you place a droplet of pond water under a microscope, an amazing

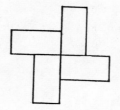

Figure 29: Spirolateral using FD 10 RT 90 FD 20 RT 90 FD 30 RT 90

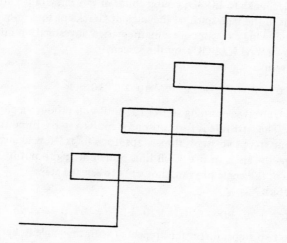

Figure 30: Spirolateral using FD 10 RT 90 FD 20 RT 90 FD 30 RT 90
FD 40 RT 90

Figure 31: A Spirolateral using RT 100

world of simple organisms is revealed. The following program is a simulation or model of animal behaviour at the level of unicellular organisms. It is what biologists refer to as stimulus-bound behaviour. I have called it BUG IN A BOX. A little animal, a paramecium, roams within a box on the screen at random. Should it touch the sides of the box, it retreats and then resumes its random movement.

In this program you will meet some new LOGO words. They are the functions XLOC and YLOC. XLOC sets the coordinates for X, the horizontal line on the screen, while YLOC sets the coordinates for the vertical. The screen is divided into a number of horizontal and vertical lines. In TANDY for example, they are 0 to 255 in the X direction and 0 to 191 in the Y direction. The lower left-hand corner of the screen has the coordinates (0, 0) while the upper right-hand corner has the coordinates (255,191). The main program is

```
TO BUG :DI :AN

PD RT RANDOM :AN

MAKE "D RANDOM :DI

CHECK

BUG :DI :AN

END
```

To start the program you need to draw a box on the screen

```
TO BOX

SX 3 SY 25

REPEAT 2 (FD 150 RT 90 FD 500 RT 90)

PU HOME PD

END
```

SX   = Set the X coordinate
SY   = Set the Y coordinate
ST   = Show turtle
HT   = Hide turtle
HOME = Position the turtle at the centre of the screen. This is X 128 and
        Y 96. The turtle heading at HOME is zero degrees or straight up.
ME is another TANDY word used with multiple turtles. It indicates the current turtle in operation. Other LOGOs do not use ME and it can be omitted.

Having drawn BOX you are ready for the main program. The aim of the program is to move the turtle at random, but with a constraint. If the turtle

approaches the set coordinates SX3 and SY 25, it should retreat. To make the
turtle do this you need a sub-procedure called CHECK.

```
TO CHECK

PU HT FD :D

IF XLOC ME <8 (BK :D)

IF XLOC ME >240 (BK :D

IF YLOC ME <30 (BK :D)

IF YLOC ME >164 (BK :D)

ELSE (BK :D ST PD FD :D)

END
```

During the running of CHECK, the turtle sometimes crosses the sides of the
box. To overcome this slight discrepancy, I have used Hide Turtle (HT). Try
running the program without HT and you will see what I mean. Perhaps you
can improve on it (figure 32).

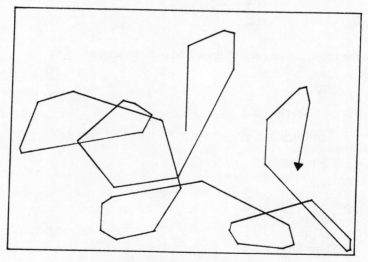

Figure 32: BUG IN A BOX

Unlike ready-made simulations in CAL programs, LOGO enables the young
learner to create his or her own simulations, directly based on laboratory
observations. The child is learning what it means to investigate a phenomenon
by making a model of it.

TREACLE HUNT

Another feature of animal behaviour essential for survival is hunting for food.
This time our animal is a fly. It buzzes about until it lands on a drop of treacle.

```
TO FLY :AN

SX 194 SY 164

HATCH1 TREACLE

LT 180

MAKE "A RANDOM :AN

HUNT

END
```

Note that TANDY LOGO does not use ('') for indicating a variable! To move
the fly around the screen you use the sub-procedure

```
TO HUNT

IF NEAR1 < 10 STOP

FD 30 RT RANDOM :A

HUNT

END
```

IF NEAR1 < 10(STOP) means that if the fly (the master turtle) is less than 10
steps away from turtle 1, then stop the program. NEAR returns a measure of
the distance from the current turtle to the one with the specified identification.
The measure is equal to the number of steps in the Y direction. If no turtle exists
with the specified identification, then the distance to HOME is measured. For
other LOGOs without multiple turtles, NEAR is equivalent to distance from a
fixed point. If you do not have the NEAR function then you must invent one for
yourself. To draw the treacle drop you need

```
TO TREACLE

SX 140 SY 96

FD 1 BK1

TREACLE

END
```

This program illustrates the use of multiple turtles. The master turtle (the one usually on the screen) is the fly, while the treacle is turtle 1. The HATCH command creates the extra turtle 1 and tells it to TREACLE. If the master turtle, alias fly, comes within a certain distance of turtle. 1, alias treacle, the program stops. There is plenty of scope for improvement here, since in TANDY LOGO you can hatch up to 250 new turtles. You could have a full-scale plague, if you so desired!

17 List Processing Projects

Creative Writing

It is important that children should become confident in handling words. They should have plenty of opportunity to consult dictionaries, reference books and, above all, novels and stories. Providing books is not too difficult, but getting the children to use them effectively is another matter. If you wish to develop your children's creative writing, then the children must learn to read with a critical mind. I found that one way to achieve this was to set up a literary data bank. With top infants (aged six to seven years) I set up a computer word bank, consisting of nouns, adjectives and verbs. Although I did not dwell on these grammatical terms, the children soon learnt to classify words under these headings.

```
TO NOUNS :PICK1

MAKE "PICK1 RANDOM 10

IF :PICK1 = 0 PRINT (CAT)

IF :PICK1 = 1 PRINT (ELEPHANT)

IF :PICK1 = 2 PRINT (DOG)

IF :PICK1 = 3 PRINT (GIRAFFE)

IF :PICK1 = 4 PRINT (COW)

IF :PICK1 = 5 PRINT (GOAT)

IF :PICK1 = 6 PRINT (MONKEY)

IF :PICK1 = 7 PRINT (DEER)

IF :PICK1 = 8 PRINT (RHINOCEROS)

IF :PICK1 = 9 PRINT (HIPPOPOTAMUS)

END
```

```
TO VERBS :PICK2

MAKE "PICK2 RANDOM 10

IF :PICK2 = 0 PRINT (IS JUMPING)

IF :PICK2 = 1 PRINT (SINGS)

IF :PICK2 = 2 PRINT (SWINGS)

IF :PICK2 = 3 PRINT (GRAZES)

IF :PICK2 = 4 PRINT (IS RUNNING)

IF :PICK2 = 5 PRINT (CHARGES)

IF :PICK2 = 6 PRINT (BARKS)

IF :PICK2 = 7 PRINT (CHIRPS)

IF :PICK2 = 8 PRINT (SWAM)

IF :PICK2 = 9 PRINT (DANCES)

END



TO ADJECTIVES :PICK3

MAKE "PICK3 RANDOM 10

IF :PICK3 = 0 PRINT (HAIRY)

IF :PICK3 = 1 PRINT (BROWN)

IF :PICK3 = 2 PRINT (SMELLY)

IF :PICK3 = 3 PRINT (BIG)

IF :PICK3 = 4 PRINT (LITTLE)

IF :PICK3 = 5 PRINT (YELLOW)

IF :PICK3 = 6 PRINT (BRAVE)

IF :PICK3 = 7 PRINT (WIDGY)

IF :PICK3 = 8 PRINT (TALL)

IF :PICK3 = 9 PRINT (FAT)

END
```

This program uses RANDOM. I have drastically modified it in order that children might write similar programs themselves. Most LOGO dialects use a more sophisticated procedure called PICKRANDOM. However it is not, in my opinion, an easy procedure to understand and for my purposes the use of RANDOM with numbers does the job reasonably well.

For older children (8 to 9 years) I wrote a program called STORY. The children collected sentences from a variety of stories, which provided them with ideas for their own use. Writing is a craft, and for children to look at what other people have done is a way of enriching their own work. It also enables them to analyse stories in a specific way. This program is also a data bank, which is divided into three sub-procedures: BEGINNINGS, PERSONS and ENDINGS.

```
TO BEGINNINGS

MAKE "TAKE1 RANDOM 10

IF :TAKE1 = 0 PRINT (ONCE UPON A TIME)

IF :TAKE1 = 1 PRINT (THERE WAS ONCE)

IF :TAKE1 = 2 PRINT (LONG AGO)

IF :TAKE1 = 3 PRINT (LATE ONE NIGHT)

IF :TAKE1 = 4 PRINT (AS JOHN WOKE UP)

          5............




TO PERSONS

MAKE "TAKE2 RANDOM 10

IF :TAKE2 = 0 PRINT (CINDERELLA)

IF :TAKE2 = 1 PRINT (THE GIANT)

IF :TAKE2 = 2 PRINT (SHERLOCK )

IF :TAKE2 = 3 PRINT (BRIAN)

IF :TAKE2 = 4 PRINT (PHOEBE DUCK)

          5..............

END
```

```
TO ENDINGS

MAKE "TAKE3 RANDOM 10

IF :TAKE3 = 0 PRINT (AND SO TO BED)

IF :TAKE3 = 1 PRINT (LIVED HAPPILY EVER AFTER)

IF :TAKE3 = 2 PRINT (RODE OFF INTO THE SUNSET)

        3...............
```

I would like to stress that it is the activity generated by this program that is of importance, rather than the contents. Children making this program are motivated to look at stories and collect useful phrases. They are learning to be critical and are enriching their own language at the same time.

Artificial Intelligence

In the USA, Professor Joseph Weizenbaum invented an interactive program called ELIZA in which the computer appeared to carry on a conversation with the operator. The computer in fact did not understand what the human operator was saying, but responded by using random phrases stored in the program. With due respect to Professor Weizenbaum and other notable researchers, my program SMALLTALK1 attempts to demonstrate the principles involved in ELIZA and other similar interactive programs.

```
TO SMALLTALK1

PRINT (MY NAME IS MAX.   WHAT'S YOURS?)

PRINT SE (I'M PLEASED TO MEET YOU) REQUEST

PRINT (HOW OLD ARE YOU?)

PRINT (SE (IT'S GOOD TO BE ) REQUEST (I AM ONLY ONE YEAR

OLD))

PRINT (TYPE SOMETHING YOU LIKE)

PRINT SE (I'M GLAD YOU LIKE) REQUEST

PRINT (HAVE YOU GOT A BROTHER?)

MAKE "ANSWER1 REQUEST
```

```
IF :ANSWER1 = (NO) PRINT (NOR HAVE I, BUT I'VE  GOT

QUITE A FEW ELECTRONIC COUSINS)

PRINT (HAVE YOU GOT A SISTER?)

MAKE "ANSWER2 REQUEST

IF :ANSWER2 = (NO) PRINT (NOR HAVE I, BUT THERE IS A

DISC DRIVE WHO IS A DISTANT RELATIVE)

PRINT (WHAT'S YOUR FAVOURITE COLOUR?)

PRINT SE (HOW ABOUT THAT!) REQUEST PRINT ( IS MY

FAVOURITE COLOUR TOO)

PRINT (I HAVE ENJOYED MEETING YOU.  WOULD YOU LIKE

TO TALK AGAIN SOME TIME?)

MAKE "ANSWER3 REQUEST

IF :ANSWER3 = (NO) PRINT (NEVER MIND. IT'S TIME FOR LUNCH

ANYWAY.  WE'VE GOT CHIPS AND CURRENTS TODAY!) ELSE PRINT

(I WOULD LIKE  THAT VERY MUCH.  BYE FOR NOW!)

END
```

The word REQUEST is a very useful tool for writing interactive programs. It waits for you to type in a line and then outputs it as a list (see chapter 14).

```
TO SMALLTALK2

PRINT (MY NAME IS MAX.  WHAT'S YOURS?)

MAKE "ANSWER1 REQUEST

PRINT SE(HELLO) :ANSWER1 PRINT (PLEASED TO HAVE

YOU AT MY KEYBOARD)

PRINT (TYPE SOMETHING YOU LIKE)

MAKE "REPLY REQUEST

MAKE "CHAT RANDOM 6
```

```
IF :CHAT = 0 PRINT SE (I'M GLAD YOU LIKE):REPLY

IF :CHAT = 1 PRINT SE (PERSONALLY, I DON'T LIKE) :REPLY

IF :CHAT = 2 PRINT SE (A LOT OF PEOPLE LIKE) :REPLY

IF :CHAT = 3 PRINT SE (YOU MUST BE CRAZY LIKING) :REPLY

IF :CHAT = 4 PRINT SE (THAT'S FUNNY, THE LAST PERSON

LIKED) :REPLY

IF :CHAT = 5 PRINT SE (I PREFER FISH AND CHIPS TO) :REPLY

PRINT SE (GOOD BYE FOR NOW) :ANSWER1

END
```

SMALLTALK2 uses random responses to simulate an 'intelligent' conversation. You can use as many phrases as you wish. All you have to do is to use RANDOM followed by a number to indicate how many phrases you have chosen. The MAKE statement with a variable such as "CHAT includes the phrases in the main program.

Conclusion

Implications of the Micro

Not only are we witnessing a technological revolution brought about by the computer, but we are also entering a new era of educational thinking. If we look for a moment at the foundation of school mathematics for example, we find that it is based on formal logic. This has resulted over the years in mathematics becoming separated and isolated from other subjects. Maths versus English, or Maths versus Art seems to be the norm in our educational system. However the computer is already beginning to change this approach to learning. No longer is the micro in schools the sole preserve of the Maths department. The micro is being used for English lessons, in learning foreign languages, and in the Art Room. Computational ideas are finding their way into all areas of the curriculum.

Let us return to mathematics. Formal logic has been the basis of School Maths with the result that extra-logical ideas such as intuition, beauty or simply pleasure, have been ignored in mathematics, save by a few enthusiastic teachers. Beauty in particular has been regarded as the icing on the cake rather than the driving force behind mathematics. Jasmin enjoys drawing and painting, and she is quite competent in Turtle Geometry. Her number work on the other hand is poor. She does not enjoy calculations and gets easily confused. Through work on the computer however, she is now beginning to realise that Maths is not just number crunching but involves other things that she can understand. If art in school was presented mainly as a collection of slightly related techniques and manipulations, then children like Jasmin would be struggling to learn how to mix paints or sharpen pencils. School Maths is still unfortunately a process by which we ask children to forget their natural experience of mathematics and learn a formal set of rules instead.

A new approach to learning is being developed by means of the computer. It is being developed through a new science called Artificial Intelligence. This science is, broadly speaking, the building of machines to do things that would require intelligence if done by people. Researchers in Artificial Intelligence have built robots that can talk, recognise photographs, and learn simple tasks. They have also produced machines that can program other machines, thus reducing the need for human intervention. Artificial Intelligence is not only an advanced form of engineering, it is also a science of learning. In order to make machines that can learn, researchers looked at learning itself. They studied educational psychology and discovered that effective learning was done procedurally. There was a parallel to be drawn between ideas in programming and the way that children learn. Seymour Papert in particular found that learning could be explained in terms of computational methods. Successful learning depends on having your knowledge highly organised and structured. By learning to program you can learn about your own thinking. This is very important as regards failure in school. Computational learning sees teaching and learning not as a matter of being wrong or right, but rather as a process of debugging. Learning through procedural thinking helps you to regard mistakes as natural. There is no feeling of shame because you cannot do something. In the area of School Maths, the micro is beginning to liberate children from the constraints of formal logic and a sense of failure. Papert goes on to say that such diverse activities as juggling and writing are connected. The processes are the same, only the end product is different. People from all disciplines should be able to find a common ground through the use of the computer. By creating a learning environment in which we emphasise the process — that is, procedural thinking — we can give people with different skills and interests something to talk about. However to make computing effective, we must recast existing knowledge, be it mathematics, science or languages, into new forms. We must not use the computer to reinforce old methods, but to reform teaching itself.

Friend or Foe?

From an educational point of view these are exciting times. The computer is a means of liberation. It transcends subject barriers and makes knowledge personal; it makes learning enjoyable, challenging and self-motivating. But what effect is the computer having on society as a whole?

One of the highlights of a BBC *Horizon* programme on Artificial Intelligence was the bizarre notion that computers of the future will regard man as an amiable pet! Ultra-intelligent machines could take over human affairs such as decision-making and scientific research. We humans could be left out in the cold. We could be slaves to electronic Frankenstein-monsters, the creations of our own intelligence. It may read like an episode from a science fiction story, but the reality of a totally computerised society is not so far away. In medicine today, computers are used as psychotherapists, and can carry out the diagnosis of certain illnesses. They are used in defence systems and in the processing of police files. Their uses are both beneficial and ominous. All the achievements of information technology are fine, provided that people are still in control. An extreme example of computer autonomy is the story about bombing raids in Vietnam, which were exclusively computer controlled. The targets for bombing were selected by machine and not by the military commanders. There is also evidence to suggest that certain pieces of data were falsified in order to procure more armaments for the war. Innocent civilians were killed. Many neutral villages were destroyed. Who was responsible, the generals or the computer? No-one seemed to know who wrote the program and furthermore no-one knew how to change it. Is this a case of blindly going by the book or rather by the machine?

While some computer scientists believe that there is nothing a computer cannot do, others see limitations on moral and cultural grounds. When John McCarthy, the inventor of LISP, the language of Artificial Intelligence, was asked if there was anything that a computer could not do, he replied that there was not.

A computer is precise and consistent. It is not partial and is seldom prone to error. Why not let a computer preside over legal matters? The problem here is that such human characteristics as love, compassion or justice cannot be computerised. Scientists like McCarthy see man in terms of a sophisticated machine. This view of man is not new. During the last century, Feuerbach wrote 'we are what we eat', namely man is nothing but an organic machine. This mechanistic view of life has also made its impact on education through the behavourists, whereby the child is seen as a machine to be conditioned by a specific teaching process.

Is the computer therefore a potential threat? What will happen to those children who are denied the use of computers in their learning? Will they be slaves to the new technology?

What of the Future?

Sean, Jasmin and other microchildren will, it is hoped, go on to greater things. By the time that they leave school they should be fairly computer literate. Perhaps they will become the designers and planners of the future. Unlike their school friends who have not had experience of LOGO, they may be in a position to shape their own future.

Surely all children should be given the opportunity to use the computer in a creative way? I personally feel optimistic about this. There will, I believe, be a marked increase in the use of computers in both primary and secondary schools. However a great amount of learning, and in particular programming, will take place in the home. It is of course difficult to foresee exactly how our children will be affected by the computerised society of the future. What is important is that the use of computers should become more widespread. This in itself may help to avert the establishment of a computer elite, the 'Masters' who are the only ones to understand computation. If we are not careful, there is a real danger of creating an authoritarianism based on expertise. The computer together with an oligarchy of experts could enslave the rest of us. As teachers and parents we must always be mindful of the limitations of the computer as well as its immense power.

Perhaps if our children learn now to program and through LOGO to teach the computer, rather than be taught or conditioned by it, they will be in a position to control the technology of the future. For LOGO is not just another computer language, it is more — it is a control language that can be applied to modern technology. Programming in the future will be written in LOGO-style languages. I believe that the future technology will be controlled by those who know LOGO and its subsequent derivatives. Furthermore, children learning LOGO now are not only becoming familiar with the ideas of computing, but they are also learning to think. LOGO teaches them to tackle such negative concepts as failure and ignorance in a logical and imaginative way.

To acquire knowledge *and* be a successful learner depends on having your own knowledge highly organised and structured. This can be put into effect at the pre-school level by using LOGO. By providing your child with the tools of the future — that is, the ideas of LOGO — you are giving him or her an opportunity to shape his or her own future. Which will your child be, an operator or a thinker?

Appendix 1: Play Turtle

Play Turtle

Before children are introduced to the floor or the screen turtle it is a good idea for them to play being the turtle themselves.

Total Turtle Trip (Theorem)
If you move from HOME, a starting point, by a succession of FORWARDS and LEFTS/RIGHTS, and continue until you end up in your original position, then the number of turns you have used always adds up to 360 degrees or a multiple of this value.

Here are some lessons I use with my children in the classroom and at home. They are recorded on workcards for the children to use by themselves.

Lesson 1
Can you move the turtle (that is, the boy/girl) round the classroom safely? Use only Turtle Talk — that is, the LOGO commands

FORWARD   LEFT
BACKWARD RIGHT

Lesson 2
Walk a square. Now walk an oblong. Write down your program. Try it on the computer!

Lesson 3
Ask your turtle (a friend) to walk a circle. Turtle must say what it is doing. Write down what happened.

Lesson 4
Turn the turtle using

```
LT 90

LT 180

LT 270

LT 360
```

Move the turtle using

```
FD :SOMETHING
```

Then

```
RT 90 RT 180 RT 270 RT 360
```

Lesson 5: Obstacles
Make your turtle go round some obstacles.
Remember

```
LT FD BK RT
```

Record the turtle's moves.

Lesson 6
You are the turtle. Walk a circle slowly. How would you ask your computer turtle to draw a circle?

Lesson 7: Using two variables
This can be extended to include angles as well as directional steps. Move your turtle

```
FD :SOMETHING   LT :SOMETHING
```

Call out the two inputs you have chosen.

Classroom Organisation

Working with LOGO has always been, and still is, a happy venture. Children work and learn best in a stress-free environment. They learn and develop their potential in a situation that is stimulating, challenging and enjoyable.

The computer, or preferably the computers, should live in the classroom. They should be part of the furniture, and in constant use from the moment the doors open until you reluctantly have to push the last-minute programmers out of the classroom.

I find that it is better for children of the same ability — that is LOGO-wise — to work in pairs initially. This enables them to discuss ideas and help each other. Later the children can work on joint projects, such as quiz games and interactive programs, in groups of four. Individual sessions, of about 15 minutes, but at frequent intervals, are the ideal. But with only one computer in the room this is not always possible.

Computer conduct

It is also advisable to set up a computer corner or area (near a wall socket — no trailing leads please!) where you and the children can go to do your programming. Strict rules of conduct have to be agreed on. No touching plugs or sockets, especially the back of domestic TV sets. The voltage is lethal! No unauthorised use of the computer is allowed, a detail that has to be enforced in the initial stages. There is always someone who likes to interfere by pressing a few buttons in the middle of another's program. Usually after the rules have been formulated and discussed by the children, there should be very few 'incidents', if any. All of my disruptive children were in fact keen programmers and certainly did not want to jeopardise the next session at the keyboard.

I have found that the children quickly accept the rules of conduct and, after the initial novelty has worn off, soon settle down to other activities apart from computing!

Appendix 2: List Processing Activities

Many infants' teachers will be familiar with word and sentence games in which the children hold up large cards with words written on them. The teacher tells the children to move about at random until the words are mixed up. We called this in our reception class — 'Mix the mixing pot'. A child or a group of children are then asked to re-arrange the children so that a sentence is made. This game can also be used to introduce the idea of list processing.

The MAKE Game

The game starts with a group of seven children. One child is chosen to be the operator. He or she holds a card with MAKE written on it. Another child called the variable holds up a card with the name of a set on it. It could be fruit or vegetables for example. The remaining five go to a table where there is a mixed assortment of fruit and vegetable cards. These children have to choose the correct card to make a set of fruit or vegetables. The cards can either have a picture of the object or just the word. The operator lines up the other six children and the rest of the class say whether the result is correct or not (see figure 33).

Figure 33

The SENTENCE Game

Once the children have played the MAKE Game successfully a few times, you can introduce the SENTENCE Game. This time the operator holds up a card with the word SENTENCE written on it. The remaining six children, or it can be five or less, hold up cards with words written on them. The sentence can be words from a nursery rhyme or a simple instruction, such as 'Who has a birthday today?'. Two or more words written on a card are called a list, while one word on a card is called a word. The word is also preceded by ("). The operator has to make a sensible sentence (see figure 34). A further development of SENTENCE is to get the children to join arms to show that they have made a list within the list. There are no hard and fast rules governing this. I leave it to you to decide whether you make other rules or not.

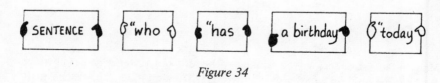

Figure 34

The WORD Game

In a similar way to the previous games, the WORD Game combines parts of words to make whole words. The rules are therefore the same (see figure 35).

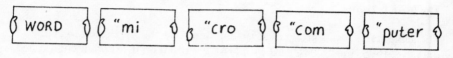

Figure 35

The CHOOSING Game

Here the children learn how to manipulate lists. The operator holds up a card with FIRST written on it. The other children in the group hold up letters — A B C D. Children from the rest of the class or group are asked to choose the correct letter. In this example it is the letter A. The child holding letter A steps forward a few paces.

The operator now changes the card to read LAST. This time the child holding the letter D card should step forward. The operator again changes the card to BUTFIRST. Children holding all but the first letter, which is A, should now step forward. Finally the operator holds up BUTLAST. Children holding A B C step forward. This game can of course be played with words and lists (see figure 36).

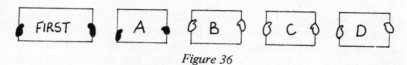

Figure 36

These games not only introduce young children to the mechanics of list processing, but they greatly aid language development. Not only do the children learn to read, but they also learn to organise their thinking by means of elementary sorting and classification.

Appendix 3: Adventure Games

Another application of list processing is the writing of adventure games. For those of you who are not familiar with this type of game, the adventure is a computer game in which you play the part of the hero or heroine. You can assume the identity of a variety of characters. You can be a crafty wizard or a daring pirate. You can be an animal or the leader of an expedition. The game takes place in a fantasy world in which you have to outwit warlocks, discover hidden treasure and fight monsters or, when I play, avoid them (!), and generally stay alive for as long as you can.

Adventure games offer an exciting and stimulating method of exploring and using language. Not only do they fire the imagination of children, but they also develop such linguistic skills as the correct use of syntax and the development of style. LOGO's friendly syntax is ideal for this type of creative writing. You can in fact write a simple, yet fascinating game, using only the MAKE statement followed by a list containing descriptive passages.

Drawing a Plan

Before writing the program in LOGO it is a good idea to draw a plan of the 'rooms' that you wish to use (see figure 37). A room in an adventure is simply a location, such as a cave, or the beach, a forest or an ogre's kitchen.

The following game called ESCAPING was written by an eight year old (it was her first attempt) and demonstrates what can be done using some elementary features of list processing.

MAKE "CASTLE (You are in a castle. You have got to get out of the castle before the Giant comes back. Which door will you choose, BLUE or GREEN?)
MAKE "BLUE (You come to two paths. Which one will you choose, LEFT or RIGHT?)
MAKE "GREEN (You find a hairy dragon. You had better go back where you came from)
MAKE "LEFT (You must find the key to the garden gate. Which way will you go, UP or DOWN?)
MAKE "RIGHT (You meet a dwarf. You must obey him. Type DWARF and you will find out what he says)
MAKE "UP (It has a horrible monster asleep. You had better type DOWN!)

Figure 37

MAKE "DOWN (You see a key. Pick it up and type GATE)
MAKE "GATE (You did not pick up the right key! You had better type RIGHT)
MAKE "DWARF (You must type GARDEN)
MAKE "GARDEN (You find the key and you must type ESCAPE)
MAKE "ESCAPE (You have escaped. How lucky you are! The End)

To run this program you type PRINT followed by each keyword in the program. Remember that MAKE with (") creates the name of a variable, while its value is preceded by (:)

MAKE "CASTLE (You are in a castle. You . . .)

To find the value of CASTLE, you type

PRINT :CASTLE

This outputs (You are in a castle . . .). Throughout this program keywords are written in capital letters, for example CASTLE, BLUE, GREEN, UP etc. Every time you type in a keyword you proceed to the next room or stage of the adventure. Thus to begin the adventure you type

PRINT :CASTLE

which tells you where you are and offers you the choice of either the blue or the green door. To chose the blue door, you type

PRINT :BLUE

To choose the green door, you type

PRINT :GREEN

and so on.

The Adventures of Poppy Brushtail

Not all adventure games however have to be of the swash-buckling variety. The next program written as a team effort with five year olds shows how almost any kind of story can be turned into an adventure. Any resemblance to a well-known story character is purely intentional!

MAKE "POPPY (You can PLAY or have your TEA)
MAKE "PLAY (You go out to play. When you are hungry type TEA)
MAKE "TEA (There are jam, butter, bread and lemonade for tea, but no ACORNS)
MAKE "ACORNS (There are some acorns in the wood, but it is dangerous there.
Do you stay at HOME or go to the WOOD?)
MAKE "HOME (Mummy Brushtail asks you to help. Choose HOUSE or GARDEN)
MAKE "WOOD (You climb trees with your sister Phil and Baby Brushtail. Go

HOME again or go FURTHER?)
MAKE "GARDEN (You do some weeding. When you have finished you ask for a
DRINK)
MAKE "HOUSE (You wash the dishes and clean the floor. When your job is done
you ask for a DRINK)
MAKE "FURTHER (A big dog chases you. You climb a tree. Phil and Baby run
home. You shout HELP)
MAKE "HELP (Daddy Brushtail finds you and brings you safely home. You ask
for a DRINK)
MAKE "DRINK (You drink a steaming hot mug of cocoa and fall asleep in your
bed)

This program runs in exactly the same way as ESCAPING. To begin type

PRINT :POPPY

and follow the choices offered by the keywords. The keyword ACORNS of
course is not a choice, it is simply a clue to the next part of the adventure. I
cannot emphasise enough how much children enjoy assuming the character of
Poppy Brushtail. It is not long before they have created a whole series of sagas,
based on popular story book characters.

Using Procedures

A more sophisticated adventure can be written using interactive procedures,
similar to those in LOGO Workshop. An adventure could begin like this

```
TO QUEST
PRINT (Who would you like to be? A King, a Queen, or a Knight?)
PRINT SE (So you are a   ) REQUEST
PRINT (You are in the garden. Which way will you go? North, South, East or
West?)
MAKE "ANSWER1 REQUEST
IF :ANSWER1 = (North) PRINT (You will meet the Ogre coming home!)
IF :ANSWER1 = (South) PRINT (You find the garden gate. Now type OPEN)
IF :ANSWER1 = (East) PRINT (You get stuck in a swamp)
IF :ANSWER1 = (West) PRINT (You fall down a deep well)
```

In this program you have an element of choice about who you will be in the
adventure as well as what to do throughout the stages of the game. The interactive feature makes the game more real especially if you provide some RANDOM
choices from within the program. You could adapt the RANDOM idea from
SMALLTALK2 in LOGO Workshop. I am sure you will agree that adventure
games, even at the level of Poppy Brushtail, offer great potential for creative
writing at any age. What about an historical simulation, say based on the Tudors,

or Scott's expedition to the Antarctic? Could you write an adventure in French for example or an adventure to illustrate the life of the Honey Bee?

Adventure games, thanks to LOGO enable children to use their factual knowledge in a personal and creative way.

Appendix 4: Suggested Reading

Artificial Intelligence

M.A. Boden, *Artificial Intelligence and Natural Man*, Harvester Press, Brighton, 1977.
An in-depth study of the moral, philosophical and psychological implications of AI.
J. Weizenbaum, *Computer Power and Human Reason*, Freeman, New York, 1976.
A very important book which discusses the moral implications of computers.

LOGO Philosophy

H. Abelson and A. di Sessa, *Turtle Geometry: the Computer as a Medium for Exploring Mathematics*, MIT Press, Cambridge, Massachusetts, 1981.
This is the standard text book on Turtle Geometry. It demonstrates the use of the turtle at university level.
S. Papert, *Mindstorms: Children, Computers and Powerful Ideas*, Harvester Press, Brighton, 1980.
The book on LOGO philosophy. A very powerful and thought-provoking account of new learning brought about by computers.

An important quarterly journal, which is ideal for parents and teachers interested in LOGO is *Logos*, printed and published by the British Logo User Group, c/o Shell Mathematics Centre, School of Education, Nottingham University.

Appendix 5: LOGO Implementations

The following implementations of LOGO are available in the UK.

Type: APPLE/LCSI LOGO
Machine: APPLE II (64 K), disc based.
Available from Apple dealers or from Apple (UK) Ltd, Eastman Way, Hemel Hempstead, Herts.

Type: ATARI LOGO
Machine: Atari 400 or 800 (48 K), cartridge based.
Available from Atari dealers.

Type: Terrapin LOGO
Machine: Commodore 64 (64 K), disc based.
Available from Commodore Business Machines (UK) Ltd, 675 Ajax Avenue, Trading Estate, Slough, Berks.

Type: IBM LOGO
Machine: IBM Personal Computer (128 K), disc based.
Available from IBM centres and dealers.

Type: RML LOGO
Machine: Either the 380Z (56 K), disc based or the 480Z (64 K), cartridge based.
Available from Research Machines Ltd, PO Box 75, Oxford.

Type: Sinclair LOGO
Machine: Spectrum (48 K), cassette based.
Available direct from Sinclair or dealers.

Type: TANDY LOGO
Machine: TRS Color computer (16 K), cartridge or disc based.
Although TANDY LOGO is only turtle graphics, it does have multiple turtles.
Available from TANDY centres or from TANDY (UK) Ltd, Tameway Tower, Bridge Street, Walsall, West Midlands.

Index